The STARTING PITCHER

The STARTING PITCHER
Baseball Behind the Seams

EMMIS BOOKS
1700 Madison Road
Cincinnati, Ohio 45206
www.emmisbooks.com

Library of Congress Control Number: 2005920006
ISBN 1-57860-163-0

Edited by Jack Heffron
Cover and interior design by Stephen Sullivan

"Dock Ellis and the New World Order" originally appeared in
Chin Music #7

Photos courtesy of Mark Rucker and Transcendental Graphics
except where indicated.
Cover photo © John Gress/Reuters/Corbis

The STARTING PITCHER

Baseball
Behind The Seams

ROB TRUCKS

CINCINNATI, OHIO

DEDICATION

For Dock Ellis, Bruce Kison and John Candelaria

And most especially for Taylor Phillips, member of the 1957
World Champion Milwaukee Braves, and perpetually
hospitable human being

THANKS

Thanks, of course, to all the pitchers who so generously
provided time, conversation and insight.

Thanks, also, to the fine folks at Emmis Books,
Angela Parker, Kevin Behan of the Baltimore Orioles,
Luis Garcia of the San Diego Padres, Jay Alves of the Colorado
Rockies, Greg Casterioto and Leigh Tobin of the Philadelphia
Phillies, Blake Rhodes and Jim Moorehead of the San Francisco
Giants, Bart Swain of the Cleveland Indians, Larry Babcock of
the Anaheim Angels, Steve Copses of the Florida Marlins,
Glenn Geffner of the Boston Red Sox, Rob Matwick and
Jimmy Stanton of the Houston Astros, Jay Horwitz,
Ethan Wilson and Chris Tropeano of the New York Mets, and
Rick Cerrone and Ben Tuliebitz of the New York Yankees.

A near bottomless pit of gratitude exists for Laurie Mundy,
the most supportive and overqualified research assistant
in history.

Very special thanks to Karan Rinaldo, Virgil Trucks,
Steve Trucks, Will Kimbrough, Inman Majors, Brian Smith,
Emilie and John Marvosa, and all who count yourselves as
family and friends.

TABLE OF CONTENTS

1st
The Pitchmaker ... *page 8*

2nd
The Rules of Pitching—A History ... *page 26*

3rd
A Pitcher's Timeline ... *page 43*

4th
A Day in the Life of a Pitcher—Andy Pettitte ... *page 55*

5th
The Craft of Pitching ... *page 85*

6th
Coaches and Catchers ... *page 103*

7th
Single-Game Starters ... *page 131*

8th
Dock Ellis and the New World Order ... *page 159*

9th
The Lists ... *page 183*

The Great Cy Young (left) with Lou Criger

1ST

The Pitchmaker

S o what does it take to be a successful pitcher in the
major leagues?

"I think that you have to be able to make pitches," says
Pat Hentgen. "You have to be a pitchmaker."

Hentgen, a fifth-round draft pick of the Blue Jays in
1986, has never been the hardest thrower in the league. But
that doesn't mean he hasn't been without success. The
right-hander is a three-time American League All-Star. He
won the Cy Young Award in 1996, ironically not one of his
three All-Star seasons. Hentgen is also an innings eater.
From 1996 to 1998 he finished in the American League's
top two for games started. In two of those three years he
led the league in innings pitched.

"Every good pitcher that I've ever played with," Hentgen says, "all had the same thing in common—they could
all spot their fastball. Jack Morris, Roger Clemens, Dave
Stieb, Dave Stewart. All the good pitchers that I've played
with could do that."

Baseball is undeniably a team sport. A twenty-five-man
roster. Nine men in the field. Nine men in the batting

order, all working (with hope) for the common good. Of those nine men in the field, the position of pitcher is without a doubt the most individualistic.

Catchers are typically six to six-feet-two inches tall with stocky bodies like bulldogs or the bulldog's friend, the fireplug. Catchers should be right-handed. While first basemen are often left-handed, they are physically larger, with comparable expectations of offensive power production. Take the same guy, make him right-handed, and put him at third.

Up the middle, the second baseman and shortstop must be quick, with good hands. Until recently, offensive production at these positions was considered icing on the cake. Outfielders can either be fast (centerfield) or powerful (most likely left). A strong arm (right) helps, and in the outfield that arm can be either left or right. Offensive production, either in terms of average or power or both, must be delivered.

But it is the pitcher, placed at the center of the infield on a throne of dirt ten inches high, who garners the most attention. The game doesn't begin until the pitcher throws toward the plate.

And pitchers, unlike other positions, come in all shapes, all sizes. Randy Johnson, who won the National League's Cy Young Award in 1999 and 2000, throws left-handed and stands 6'10" with a weight of 225 pounds. Pedro Martinez, who also brought home the Cy Young in 1999 and 2000, is right-handed and charitably listed at 5'11" and a weight of 170 pounds.

Given that pitchers seem to come in all shapes and sizes,

it seems a relatively safe assumption that starting pitchers are made, not born.

Relief pitchers, specifically with the recent development of the single inning closer, may be able to get by, even have remarkable success, with a one- or two-pitch arsenal. Yankee ace Mariano Rivera, for example, is, in all likelihood, the best at his position, and while he will, on occasion, throw both a two-seam fastball and a four-seam fastball, it is Rivera's dreaded cut fastball thrown in the low nineties, tailing in on left-handers and turning their bats into so many oversized toothpicks, that has confounded American League batters for nearly a decade.

While it may be wishful thinking, or at the very least a rarity, that a starter will face a batting order four times in the course of a game, it's disappointing if he doesn't face at least some opposing batters three times. Therefore, to be successful, a major league starting pitcher should possess a repertoire of at least three pitches he can count on.

"When I broke in," Pat Hentgen says, "my first six years I was fastball, curveball. And now I'm cut fastball, change-up, fastball, curveball. I've created two more pitches because my velocity might not be the same. I rely on my command as much as anybody in the league probably. I've changed to the point where I added two pitches, but I'm still a fastball-curveball pitcher. But now I have two more pitches so, on those days when the fastball-curveball might not be there, I've got this and I've got that.

"To go through the lineup the third and fourth time in the major leagues after they've seen you and seen every pitch that you have, now it comes down to who can command the ball and throw the ball in good areas where it's hard to center."

Sure, pitchers who stand 6'3" and throw ninety-mile-an-hour fastballs in high school are going to get the scout's attention (and the organization's money), but that doesn't guarantee major league success.

"They're only looking for potential," Bill Lee says of scouts, "and that's the main thing that's wrong with major league baseball. With the scouting procedures they bypass guys like me and Johnny Podres, you know, guys that don't really throw that hard. They're always looking for potential. They're not looking for guys that are established pitchers."

Lee, nicknamed "Spaceman," pitched in fourteen major league seasons with the Red Sox and Expos after being selected all the way down in the twenty-second round of the 1968 draft. He is both a native Californian and a lefty, two factors that, according to baseball logic, help make him one of the most quotable pitchers to ever play the game.

"I never threw hard," Lee says. "I always threw below the radar gun, but I had pinpoint control. I could throw hard when I wanted to, but I had learned to pitch. I was a pitcher right off. I was never a thrower. Most kids nowadays are throwers, and the teams say, We'll teach you how to pitch.

"I was a pitcher from the day I took the mound. I was a three-pitch pitcher by the time I was nine years old, and by the time I got to college I was cutting the ball and sinking the ball. I had two fastballs, and I had a hard breaking ball, a slow breaking ball, and I had a straight change. Well, it was a screwball change that I threw early. I didn't start throwing the circle change until I was fifty, where I am right

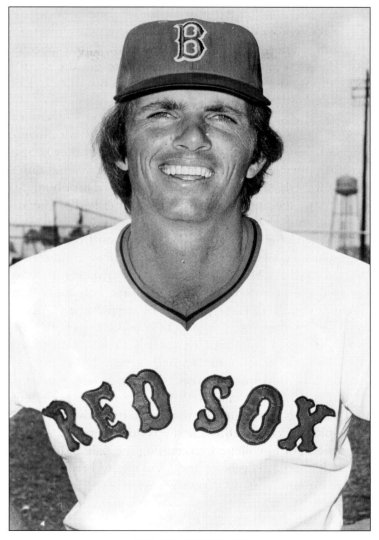

BILL "SPACEMAN" LEE

now. Now I've got two change-ups. I've got two fastballs. I've got the overhand dude, so I throw sliders occasionally to left-handers, good left-handed hitters, in tough situations when I play in these adult leagues."

Who transformed Bill Lee from thrower into pitcher at such an early age? His aunt, Annabelle Lee, the only woman to pitch a perfect game in the All-American Girls Professional League.

"My aunt was a great pitcher," says Lee, "and I must've got her genes because she couldn't hit a lick."

"The second pitch I learned how to throw was a change-up. My aunt taught me how to turn the ball over, and then I learned the overhand curve from her also. Nowadays you don't throw a curveball until your elbow matures, but I learned the correct way to throw a curveball without hurting my elbow, so I had a good curveball by the time I was nine years old."

Of course, not every prospective major league pitcher is fully developed in his talents at the age of nine. But some begin their trek at an even earlier age.

"When I was four until I was eight I was playing first and outfield off and on," say Giants right-hander Jerome Williams, "and then they converted me to a catcher because I had a pretty good arm. I was catching probably every day, and say like the end of the game they'd put me in to pitch, to shut them down. But I was mostly a catcher."

"At first I didn't want to be a catcher. I was afraid of the ball. Even with the gear and everything I was afraid of the ball. I didn't even like to block balls or anything."

Once Williams got comfortable behind the plate,

however, he quickly selected a role model—a role model, ironically enough, who would later catch Williams during his rookie season in San Francisco.

"I patterned my whole catching career after Benito [Santiago]," Williams says. "Everything he did, I did. I mean, I threw people out from my knees, had my gloves hanging out of my pocket when I was batting. Everything." Interestingly enough, it was Williams's naturally strong arm—and his father's wariness of it—that kept him from becoming a pitcher immediately.

"One coach told my dad, Try to put him on the mound. My dad knew already I had no control," Williams says. "So my dad was like, No. Don't put him on the mound. He'll hurt somebody. And he was right.

"I was known as a wild pitcher when I was younger," Williams says in an understatement.

"The first batter I faced, the first ball I threw was a fastball, and it ran in on a girl and broke her ribs. From then on he was like, He ain't pitching no more. But I wanted to try and pitch."

Phillies pitcher Randy Wolf is another who played behind the plate before he played on the mound.

"I played shortstop, and I caught," Wolf says.

An All-Star selection in 2003, Wolf's participation at short and catcher is even more remarkable considering he's a left-hander.

"You could get away with a lot in Little League," he says.

Wolf's former teammate Kevin Millwood began his playing career in the outfield, primarily because he was younger than most of the boys on his team.

"It was the first year I'd ever played baseball," Millwood says. "It was the first year I'd done anything organized like that, and I just wanted to have fun. Then the next year I played again and got a chance to start playing a little bit more, and I enjoyed it.

"I don't really remember what happened to make me become a pitcher, but I always threw the ball pretty hard, and anybody who throws the ball a little bit hard in Little League gets a chance to pitch. I just wanted to play, and when I played I got a chance to pitch."

Jake Peavy begins his fourth season in the majors in 2005, but the twenty-three-year-old Alabama native has already seen success. With a fastball in the low- to mid-nineties, Peavy averaged more than a strikeout an inning in 2004 and led all National League starters in ERA with a mark of 2.27.

"I guess I was probably five or six," Peavy says, "and Dad took me down to Municipal Park there in Mobile and we started playing. I played everything growing up—baseball and football and church league basketball. I played all three sports all the way up through high school, and I've been playing baseball as long as I can remember."

Peavy's talent on the baseball field was easily recognized.

"I was a pitcher," he says. "Obviously everybody knew that I had a God-given talent to throw a baseball hard."

Like Peavy, Pirates starter Kip Wells is a right-hander who throws in the low- to mid-nineties. Like Peavy, Wells, a first-round draft pick by the White Sox in 1998, was brought to the game by his dad, a former college pitcher at the University of Texas.

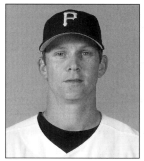

KIP WELLS

"He didn't push me to play until I was ready," Wells says of his father, "so I didn't start until I was twelve. He said that whenever I wanted to play I could play, and before that he didn't really make me or ask me."

Like his father, Wells was a pitcher from the very beginning.

"I played the field when I didn't pitch," he says, "but he told me if I was going to make a living in this business it'd be on the mound. I mean, I had a good arm.

"I'm sure you can get comparable coaching from your high school coach or your college coach," Wells says, "or you might get lessons or something, but having a father that pitched just kind of cuts out the middle man. Even to this day, he still thinks he knows a lot about pitching."

Wells's dad watches his starts via satellite and often calls his son with suggestions.

"He's never overly aggressive or negative with me," Wells says. "It's always constructive. But still, regardless of whether it's your father or somebody else, if you're watching the game from the outside, and you're not on the mound, you can make different observations. It's like, The guy looks like he's rushing, or, The guy looks like he's slowing down his mechanics on his pitches or whatever—things you can only observe from the side.

"But having him as a father allowed me to mature as far as how to do it. Not that I did it the right way all the time,

16

but I knew that mechanics were important. Changing speeds, moving the ball around, all that stuff. It wasn't my first year in Little League when I was throwing to the corners with breaking balls or anything, but still he got me started in the right direction."

Cincinnati native Zach Day grew up a die-hard Reds fan. Although third baseman Chris Sabo was his boyhood idol, Day, with the help of his father, took to the mound immediately.

"My dad was always my coach when I was growing up," he says, "and I think the first year we started to have pitchers that's when I started pitching. I played a little outfield, a little shortstop, but other than that it was my number-one thing. The best thing I was able to do was pitch, and so that's always something I've done ever since. It's all I've known."

Boston starter Bronson Arroyo's father played an even more active role in his young son's baseball development.

"My dad recognized the first year I played tee-ball at five years old that I was a little bit better than most of the kids out there," Arroyo says, "and from that point on he pretty much raised me to be a ballplayer.

"He didn't have much of a baseball background but was more into weight training actually. He was a friend of a power lifter, so I started lifting weights when I was about six years old and just kind of went that way and then developed over the years more into the baseball area.

"I begged him to let me play tee-ball my first year, and so they took me out there and he just saw a natural gift in me. I picked the ball up and threw it and ran and fielded so much better than all the other kids my age that he just thought we better take it and run with this. I started lifting and throwing and hitting. He got me a batting machine and a batting cage and I started hitting and throwing and running and taking ground balls. All the things that we do now as a major league baseball player I've been doing my whole life."

Arroyo, a third-round selection by the Pirates in 1995, has no regrets about his regimen as a youngster.

"I don't know if I would've played in the major leagues if it hadn't been for my father training me the way he did," he says. "I definitely think it worked. It gave me the strength. It gave me a lot of stamina. I've never been on the disabled list. I've been healthy my whole career. I think him doing these things with me definitely gave me a good foundation."

Find a weekend jogger and his or her closet will almost certainly contain more than one pair of running shoes. At some point the beginning runner says to himself, A new pair of shoes will make me a better runner. The same compulsion inhabits the novice pitcher, no matter the talent level. Of course, no one wants to deny an aspiring runner that new pair of shoes, or that aspiring pitcher another pitch, but the decision often comes down to want versus need.

Jim Kaat pitched twenty-five big league seasons. He retired with a total of 283 career victories. He pitched in two World Series and won 20 games or more in a season three times. Kaat won a record-setting 16 consecutive Gold Glove Awards and at some point in his career led the league in wins, winning percentage, games started, innings pitched, complete games, and shutouts. After retiring Kaat served as a major league pitching coach, and he now works as a color commentator for the New York Yankees.

Few men alive have seen as many major league ball-games as Jim Kaat, and he believes that control, rather than the number of pitches in a young pitcher's arsenal, is what's truly important.

"I'm sort of old school from the standpoint that I still think the best way to develop some arm strength and find the rhythm and the flow of the motion is by throwing the ball," Kaat says. "Warren Spahn gave me a good exercise, and I still pass it on to a lot of young pitchers. You go out in centerfield, and you pick up a ball that's on the ground. You take that hop and step like an outfielder. You're going to one-hop it into second base. That's really how you find your natural motion.

"With the young pitcher you'd like to find a motion and a release point, an arm slot where out of ten fastballs he can throw nine of them in the strike zone. Maybe he can end up getting ten. Then he can work on getting five on the outside half and five on the inside half from that same arm slot."

All, of course, before the young pitcher develops a second pitch.

Ask a current major league pitcher what was the second pitch he learned to throw and nine of ten will say "curveball." Ask a major league pitcher what second pitch he would teach his son, and nine of ten will say "change-up."

"I think that's the best pitch in baseball right now," says

JIM KAAT

the Giants Jason Schmidt. "A lot more guys are starting to throw it. I like it better than the breaking ball. Not because of the arm, but I just think it's an easier pitch to throw."

Kip Wells agrees. "I probably went fastball to a curveball. But at this day and age, to keep pressure and strain off your arm, I think the change-up."

Of the curve, Wells says, "Every kid wants to be able to see the ball do that, but if you can get them to at least start tinkering with a change-up and realizing that it has a similar effect that the curveball has except it doesn't break as much. It's just a change of speed. It allows a kid that's young to figure out that changing speeds is important, and not just throwing fastballs and snapping off curveballs."

Still shy of thirty-two, pitcher Shawn Estes already has ten National League seasons to his credit.

"I've been a pitcher from day one," he says, "from the time I was probably nine years old. From the time I picked up a baseball I just knew I had a good arm, and, at that age, I could always throw harder than most of the kids my age, so that related to being a pitcher. The harder the better."

Though not known as a hard thrower in the majors, Estes was a first-round draft pick of the Seattle Mariners in 1991.

"Throwing a baseball overhand is probably the most unnatural motion you could do," Estes says. "You shouldn't be doing it. But the older you get the smarter you get with how you actually throw a baseball overhand. I was a maximum-effort guy from the time I was nine years old. When I picked up a baseball I threw as hard as I could.

"But I'm still becoming a pitcher. Getting hurt helps you

become a pitcher, too, because you can't rare back and throw it as hard as you want to throw it, with consistency. In the minor leagues that's all I did. I walked a lot of guys and I struck out a lot of guys, and I ended up giving up a lot of runs in the process. I didn't learn until later on that I don't have to throw it as hard as I can to have success. And still I battle with it. There are times in a game when I try to throw it as hard as I can, you know what I mean? But I'm a little bit more in control of that when I do it now, and I realize that's not the way to go about it. One, I might get hurt, or two, I'm not going to have as much consistency, so I've learned how to back off at times, and I've also kept a little bit extra for when I need it. But I still battle with it every time I take the mound.

"It's a learning process of what you can and can't do," Estes says, "and through trial and error learning what you can and can't do—by making mistakes, realizing that's not the way to do it. Like getting hurt, realizing that's not the way to do, and just trying to find your niche. At thirty-one I'm finally finding my niche, because I've been caught in between my whole career, being healthy and hurt, being healthy and hurt, being hard and soft. I didn't know what I was as a pitcher."

Although it would be too broad a statement to suggest that every man who throws a baseball from a mound must be injured in order to make the transition from thrower to pitcher, the cause and effect of the phenomenon is not unheard of.

Al Leiter, a second-round draft pick of the Yankees back in 1984, is as close to a pitching physicist as you will find on a current major league staff. Though he didn't reach 60 innings pitched in any of his first six major league campaigns, he begins the 2005 season, his nineteenth as a big leaguer, as a member of the Florida Marlins. His education, he says, didn't come until after he was injured as a professional.

"In Little League, I threw the ball by most all the hitters and then, obviously, I wasn't aware of the physics involved.

"I actually found out I was doing it wrong," Leiter says. "That I was compensating because of the strength that I had, God-given, and I ended up having two shoulder surgeries. After my second shoulder surgery in '91, I basically revamped my pitching mechanics to put less strain on my shoulder and elbow. My understanding of the core came in winter of '91, and getting to a delivery that puts less strain in my arm.

"Legs are important," he says. "Legs and midsection are important for a pitcher. The core of the pitching motion starts from the center of your body out, and as a pitcher you concentrate most on your abs, your gluts, and your quads and hamstrings. If the core is stronger, then when it gets to your shoulder and elbow and wrist and knees and ankles, as a result of having a stronger core it puts lesser strain on your weaker muscles.

"If you take the pitching mechanics," Leiter says, "you have to think of it in terms of physics. There's a lot of timing and angles in which you maximize your ability to throw a ball harder based on, basically, a slingshot mentality of a fulcrum and a sling. You're coiled in the right position at the right time with your arm in the right position, everything uncoiling, and it gives you, hopefully, the maximum arm speed with your arm in position to give you the right angle and the extension that's needed."

Like most pitchers who have suffered close calls with their careers due to injury, Leiter advises caution for young pitchers, particularly in the area of weight lifting.

"Allow nature to take its course before you start trying to increase muscle mass on a physique that perhaps may not be able to take it," he says. "That's when ligament and tendon problems occur. That's the whole thing with steroid use—guys have the frame of what God gave them, of say a 185-200-pound person, and then when one takes steroids and now they're 225-230, the muscles grow but the tendons and joints still think and feel and want to be 185."

Jason Schmidt of the Giants has truly come into his own in the past two seasons. He was selected to the National League All-Star team in both 2003 and 2004. In each of the past two seasons he finished in the top four in National League Cy Young voting. In each of the past two seasons he has finished in the top four in wins, the top five in winning percentage, the top eight in ERA, the top two in hits allowed per nine innings, the top five in strikeouts per nine innings, the top four in overall strikeouts, and the top four in complete games. And in each of the past two seasons Jason Schmidt has led the National League in shutouts.

The most important lesson that he's learned as a professional?

"I think the main thing for me," he says, "is composure. I always had the hardest time, when I was young, having composure on the mound. You see a young guy give up a hit, swearing on the mound, kicking dirt. Next pitch he tries to throw it harder, gives up another hit, comes into the dugout, throws his glove. I'm not like that. But that used to be my biggest problem coming through the minor leagues. "The biggest thing," he says, "and everybody's heard this, is anybody should be able to turn their TV on at any given time, and if they don't see the score they should be able to look at your face and not tell who's winning or losing."

"Give up a hit? You're going to give up a hit. It's not going to be the first one, and it's not going to be the last one, so go out there and pitch as good as you can. You're going to give up your hits. You're going to win some and you're going to lose some. Just take your lumps as they come. And that's what I've done."

It all comes down, however, to making pitches.

Starting pitcher, Pat Hentgen reminds us, is "not a power position. It's more of a finesse-type skill position. It's a feel position. You don't just stand on the mound and get all excited and throw the ball as hard as you can. Very few guys can do that, and if they do they're probably not going to be successful for any length of time. You might be successful for a season or two seasons, but like I said, spot your fastball. That's the number one piece of advice I could give any young pitcher."

2ND

The Rules of Pitching—A History

Ask Bill "Spaceman" Lee the last time professional baseball instituted a rule change that benefited his brethren pitchers and you'll get a firm answer: "Never," Lee says. "They never have. If you look back at the old baseball magazines by Spalding back in 1918, every time they tried to lessen the pitcher because they wanted more offense. They've been doing that eternally. They say they're going to help the pitcher but they never do because, the thing is, umpires are closer to the hitter than they are to the pitcher. They're there, right there, and they get intimidated by hitters. And pitchers are a long ways away."

Baseball rules, of course, are not set by umpires, but rather the Baseball Rules Committee, subject to owner approval. You might call the Rules Committee baseball's legislative branch. They pass the laws. Call the umpires the judicial branch. They get to interpret the law (especially in the case of the strike zone). So while the Spaceman may not be literally correct, he's certainly leaning in the right direction.

Throughout baseball's storied history, rules have been made and broken, emphasized and ignored, adopted and amended. And in almost every instance, particularly since 1919, the resulting change has favored the batter, because if the career of one George Herman "Babe" Ruth taught baseball's owners anything, it was that offense sells.

In 1882, the Cincinnati Red Stockings bested a six-team American Association field comprised of the Philadelphia Athletics, Louisville Eclipse, Pittsburgh Alleghenys, St. Louis Brown Stockings and the woeful Baltimore Orioles (the team went 19 and 54 for a .260 winning percentage) in the league's initial season. But American Association pitchers of that time bore little resemblance to today's major league moundsmen.

To begin with, there was no mound. Pitchers were forbidden to throw the ball overhand. They stood just fifty feet from home plate in a six-foot square box. For a time, not unlike a schoolyard kickball game, batters could call for a specific delivery—high, low or fair (right down the middle). The man in the pitcher's box more closely resembled a first-year Little League coach gently lofting the ball toward a toddler's bat than, say, Randy Johnson, as the function of the pitcher was to simply put the ball in play.

Obviously little attention was paid to the hurler's competitive nature. Soon, however, pitchers collectively cried, Enough! Whereas baseball's original intent was to have the ball sail softly toward the plate with an underhanded, locked-wrist delivery (deliveries above the pitcher's waist were not allowed), pride set in. Pitchers began changing speeds. Arms began flailing outward from the body (not unlike a Gene Garber or Dan Quisenberry) in an attempt to gain speed and alter trajectory. The locked-wrist rule was quickly ignored, and various grips and spins on the ball were used in an attempt to confuse the batter.

Pitcher Will White of the 1882 Cincinnati Red Stockings is not only the first major leaguer to wear eyeglasses on the field, but also purportedly the first major league pitcher to master the curveball. Before the American Association's inception, White had played for the National League's Cincinnati Reds, Boston Beaneaters and Detroit Wolverines, but in 1882 White was definitely the new league's star pitcher. Though White finished fourth in ERA (1.54) before claiming the title the following season, he led the league in wins (40—10 more than his next closest competitor), winning percentage (.769), complete games (52 of his 54 starts), shutouts (8) and innings pitched (an astounding 480, which nevertheless pales in comparison to the major league record 680 innings he pitched in the National League three years earlier).

By 1884, the American Association had expanded to thirteen teams, the National League claimed eight teams and the Union Association, made up of twelve franchises, played its one and only season. Pitchers caught a break when all restrictions on their delivery were removed, ostensibly allowing them to throw overhand for the first time. This isolated swing in the pitcher's favor most likely occurred simply because the old rules (such as the locked-wrist delivery) were deemed unenforceable. Pitchers still threw from just fifty feet away, and with a new variety of available deliveries, it's rather amazing that baseball showed any offense at all.

It was not until 1893, two years after the American Association had gone out of business, leaving the National as the sole major league, that rule changes truly turned against the pitcher in what would be the beginning of a long shift in momentum. The year that the Boston Beaneaters claimed their third consecutive National League crown, the pitcher's box was not only eliminated, but replaced by a rubber slab measuring twelve by four inches. Most importantly, however, the newly created rubber was placed not fifty feet from home plate as it had been the previous year, but at a more batter-friendly distance of sixty feet six inches, where it remains today.

Offensive statistics skyrocketed with the additional ten feet. The league batting average of .245 in 1892 ballooned to an impressive .280. The Brooklyn Grooms' Dan Brouthers won the league batting title with a .335 average in 1892. The following season it took .380, the mark attained by the Phillies' Billy Hamilton, to lead the league. Whereas Bug Holliday was the National League's homerun champion with 13 in 1892, Billy Hamilton's Philadelphia teammate Big Ed Delahanty pounded 19 homers the following season.

Pitching statistics, too, were greatly affected by the increased distance. Cy Young of the Cleveland Spiders would pitch his team into the championship series in 1892 (they lost to Boston's Beaneaters) with a league-leading ERA of 1.93. The following season no pitcher was on the south side of two runs a game. In fact, no National League pitcher was under three runs a game as the St. Louis Browns' Ted Breitenstein's 3.18 ERA was the league's best. The added ten and a half feet also had a profound effect on a pitcher's endurance. The Chicago Colts' Bill Hutchison managed 622 pitched innings in 1892. The following year, Hall of Famer Amos Rusie would toss but 482 innings, but it would be enough to lead the league.

The National League batting average remained upward of .290 from 1894 to 1897 (actually reaching .309 in 1894 when Boston's Hugh Duffy led the league with a .440 mark). The National League ERA remained above 4.30 over those same seasons, so in 1900, in the next-to-last move that would benefit pitchers in the coming century, home plate was redesigned—from a twelve-inch square to the current five-sided figure, seventeen inches across at its widest point, that is still used today. But this would also mark the beginning of the end of rules changes that would benefit the pitcher.

In 1904 the height of the pitcher's mound, a source of great leverage, was established at fifteen inches and would remain so for the next sixty-five seasons. Pitchers ruled the roost from a perch fifteen inches high during the aptly named Deadball Era (from 1900 to 1919). The formation of the American League in 1900 (though it wasn't recognized as a "major" league until 1901) created two major leagues, and pitching ruled them both.

The American League batting average in 1901 was .277, its highest mark until 1920. Their counterparts in the

National League hit their peak in 1912 (when the league experimented with a livelier ball) with a .272 average. From 1901 to 1919, pitching records were even more remarkable. The major league ERA leader from 1901 to 1919 managed a mark of less than 2.0 runs a game in every single season. In only one campaign, 1911 when Vean Gregg's 1.80 mark led the league, did the league leader's ERA rise to even 1.55, and in 1914 Dutch Leonard held opposing hitters to less than one run a game with an ERA of 0.96.

The reason was the spitball.

Of course, "spitball" was a more or less all-encompassing term used to cover all manner of doctoring a baseball. The ball could be scraped with an emery board or a file, lubricated with spit, tobacco juice or an otherwise unappetizing combination. Slippery elm or chewing gum could be applied to help alter the ball's path to the plate. Any imperfection to the ball's assumed circumference would help to create a hiccup or break in its trajectory—and give hitters fits.

In the Deadball Era, everyone threw the spitball, whether they wanted to or not.

Imagine going to the gym, and coming out of the shower to discover there is but one community towel. Not very appealing, I know, but major league games in 1914 were not stocked with three dozen brand new baseballs. Balls were used until they were too dirty to be seen. If the opposing pitcher threw a spitball, then by default you did too.

Perhaps the most famous practitioner of the shine ball (a spitball subset) was Eddie Cicotte, best known as one of

the eight players banned from baseball by Commis-
sioner Kennesaw Mountain Landis for his participation in
the 1919 Black Sox Scandal. In John Sayles' movie *Eight
Men Out,* Cicotte is portrayed by actor David Straithorn
who, in full view of players, umpires and fans, "shines" the
baseball against his right pantsleg before going into his
windup. In real life the career American Leaguer garnered
a total of 40 wins versus 17 defeats in his final two seasons,
1919 and 1920 (the World Series fix was not discovered
until the following year), and he led the junior circuit in
ERA in 1917 and in Wins in both 1917 and 1919.

But in December of 1919 (after a consistent ten-year
outcry by managers of overmatched hitters, as well as a
recent nationwide flu epidemic that may well have been the
straw that broke the spitball camel's back), all "freak deliveries" in baseball were abolished. In layman's terms, this
meant no more spitballs. Or emery balls. Or shine balls.

An addendum, however, was offered. American League
pitchers designated as spitballers (there seems to be no lim-
it on the number of potential designees) could continue to
throw a doctored sphere for the rest of their career. In the
National League, each team could designate two pitchers
as spitballers. In total, seventeen pitchers were granted the
most coveted of all entitlements—License to Spit.

The last of the seventeen "designated" legal spitballers,
Burleigh Grimes, a.k.a. "Ol' Stubblebeard," threw his last
major league pitch for the New York Yankees on July 17,
1934, his first taste of the American League after eighteen
plus seasons in the National. Grimes pitched in four World

Series and won 270 regular season games in his nineteen-year career while losing 212. He led the league in Wins twice and complete games four times. Following his retirement as a player, Grimes managed the Brooklyn Dodgers in 1937 and 1938 and was elected to the Hall of Fame in 1964.

In 1919, the ERA for American League pitchers was 3.22. The next year it would rise to 3.79 and by 1921, just the second year after the spitball was banned, American League pitchers were allowing 4.28 runs a game—an increase of a full run in just two seasons. National League pitchers were similarly flummoxed. In 1919, the league ERA stood at 2.91 (the last season in either league's history that a league ERA would end up under three runs a game). In 1920 it rose to 3.13, to 3.78 in 1921 before reaching 4.10 in 1922—over a full run increase in three seasons.

Of course, 1919 was also the first full season in the outfield, and the last in a Red Sox uniform, for a former pitcher by the name of Babe Ruth. He hit 29 homeruns for his second homerun title. But those 29 homeruns were nearly three times more than the 10 hit by second place finisher Frank "Home Run" Baker. Ruth would go on to win ten more league homerun titles (and many more in other categories besides), and while there probably should've been a rules change for pitchers facing the Sultan of Swat, baseball's newly found offense drew paying crowds in record numbers, owners danced a fat and happy, full pockets jig, and baseball's tenuous balance between pitcher and hitter was shifted forever.

* * * * *

And then . . . nothing happened.

Actually that's what your mom might call a fib, what your ex-wife (or her appointed legal representative) might call a bald-faced lie rendered with malice and forethought. But for forty-eight years, changes to the rulebook that directly affected pitchers were minimal.

There were minor additions, of course. Pitchers were granted permission to use a resin bag in 1925. In 1939 and '40 there were small, technical notations dealing with the pitcher's foot, the rubber, and how much contact and movement might be allowed. In 1950 the rulebook took the time to restate the approved height of the mound (still 15 inches), but it wasn't what you could call a rule change.

In 1955 a regulation was created in one of baseball's everlasting efforts to speed up the game. The additional dictum dictated that if any base was occupied by a runner, then the pitcher must deliver the pitch within twenty seconds of receiving the ball from the catcher or the umpire may call a ball. Either this rule has been completely ignored, or I missed the amendment that nullified its effectiveness any time a pitcher named Trachsel took the mound.

And then . . . 1968.

That was The Year of the Pitcher, a time of light-headed wonderment and awe for all who aspire to one day reign as King of the fifteen-inch Hill. Despite American League expansion in 1961 and National League expansion in 1962 (general wisdom believing that expansion in any year effectively waters down pitching staffs moreso than offensive capability), in the 1960s pitching became a power game and pitchers had the power.

From 1962 through 1967, ERAs plummeted. The highest mark for either league's leader in this span was a relatively tame 2.54 by Sandy Koufax in 1962. American League batters managed an average better than .250 just once in this period. National League batters managed the feat only twice.

After nearly a decade of imbalance in the pitcher's favor, the trend reached its apex in 1968 when Bob Gibson led National League starters with a 1.12 ERA. Luis Tiant of Cleveland led American Leaguers with a 1.60 total. Not since 1917 had the two league ERA leaders combined for a sum total of less than three runs per game. And it hasn't happened since.

The earned run average for all American League pitchers in 1968 was 2.98, the first time the total came in under three runs since 1918. This hasn't happened since (4.63 was the mark in 2004). The earned run average for all National League pitchers was also 2.98, the first time the total came in under three runs since 1919. And, of course, it hasn't happened since.

In 1968 Boston's Carl Yastrzemski won the American League batting title with a .301 average. Not only was this the lowest batting average to win a league title in major league history, Yastrzemski's .301 remains the lowest batting average to win a league title in major league history. National League hitters swatted a mere 891 homeruns in

1968, the first season the league failed to reach at least 1000 roundtrippers since 1952.

In 1968 Detroit's Denny McLain won 31 games in the regular season, the first time a pitcher had reached 30 victories in a campaign since Dizzy Dean for the Cardinals in 1934. And given that even the most active of current major league starters rarely appear in more than 35 games in a season, McLain's win total will likely never be duplicated.

Clearly this domination, this stifling of offensive production, had to be stopped. To culminate this most pitching rich season, Mickey Lolich and Bob Gibson dueled on behalf of the Detroit Tigers and St. Louis Cardinals in the 1968 World Series. Both men started three games, recorded matching 1.67 ERAs, and though Bob Gibson set a still-standing record of 35 strikeouts in a single Series, Lolich took Game 7 for Detroit as Gibson returned on three days' rest. Changes would have to be made.

The strike zone, heretofore recognized, at least in theory, as the batter's shoulders to the bottom of his knees, was theoretically compressed (see: the judicial branch) to from the armpits to the top of the knees. The Save rule was added for the first time. But of primary importance was the lowering of the mound—from fifteen inches to ten inches—thereby reducing the pitcher's leverage.

The decrease may well have been more than 33 percent as pitching-rich teams like the Dodgers and White Sox were rumored to fashion mounds higher than the prescribed fifteen inches. Nevertheless, the lowering of the

DENNY MCLAIN

mound helped to increase the National League batting average seven points, from .243 in 1968 to .250 in 1969. American League batters combined for a whopping 16-point rise in average, from .230 in 1968 to .246 in 1969. Pitcher ERAs climbed even more significantly. Each league experienced an increase of well over a half run per game—the ERA for National League pitchers moved from 2.98 to 3.59; American League pitchers from 2.98 to 3.62.

National League run production increased an astounding 41 percent from 1968 to 1969 alone.

Of course, 1969 was also an expansion year. The National League welcomed the San Diego Padres and Montreal Expos while the American League added the Seattle Pilots and Kansas City Royals. And conventional wisdom has always advanced the argument that pitching is a commodity more rare than hitting, and that fact alone might account for at least some of the increased offense. But that reasoning doesn't necessarily hold up through history.

In 1901, when the American League was recognized as a second major league (effectively doubling the number of major league players), the National League batting average fell by eight points from the prior season. The combined ERA for National League pitchers also dropped—by more than half a run per game.

In 1961, the season of Roger Maris's 61 homers (28 more than he hit in any other year), the major leagues expanded from the sixteen-team base utilized since Maris was knee high to a grasshopper. The Washington Senators moved to Minnesota and became the Twins, a new Washington Senators franchise established residence in Griffith Stadium, and the Los Angeles Angels opened for business in the Wrigley Field of the West. The following year the National League accepted the Houston Colt .45s and New York Mets (who won but one out of every four games they played over the course of the season).

One would expect, especially in light of the anecdotal evidence of Maris's record-setting season, that offensive numbers in the first year of expansion would dwarf those of the previous season, but American League batters raised their average a mere point, from .255 to .256, from 1960 to 1961 while National League batters took a similar-sized step, but in the opposite direction. National League hitters in 1961 batted .262. In 1962 they batted just .261, and the league ERA dropped as well.

So while offensive production has certainly not reached astronomic heights, the tide had definitively turned. And as the old saying goes, Give the American League five inches and they'll take a mile. While the decision by American League owners to add the designated hitter for the start of the 1973 season didn't directly affect pitchers in the same way that, say, a reinterpretation of the strike zone or the lowering of the mound would, perhaps no other rule change in baseball history has so blatantly placed our beloved hurler in such unfavorable light.

In 1972, National League batters averaged .248 while American League hitters tallied but .239. National League teams averaged 3.91 runs per game while American League

BOB GIBSON

teams managed just under three and a half runs. New York Yankee Bobby Murcer scored 102 runs during the 1972 campaign, the only American Leaguer to cross home plate 100 times. Five National Leaguers, led by Reds second baseman Joe Morgan with 122, would score more than Murcer. A sense of imbalance, like so much rotten cheese stuck in the air conditioning, wafted through the offices of American League owners. And 1972 was exhibit A in a larger body of evidence. The National League scored more runs than its younger counterpart in every season but one since 1965. Something had to be done.

On April 6, 1973, New Yankees second baseman Horace Clarke singled to left against Boston starter Luis Tiant to lead off the game. Leftfielder Roy White then struck out in the front end of a strike 'em out, throw 'em out double play. But rightfielder Matty Alou, in his first at-bat as a Yankee, doubled. Bobby Murcer, who had finished second in the league in home runs the year before, walked. Third baseman Graig Nettles, also in his first Yankee appearance, walked to load the bases and Blomberg, the first designated hitter in major league history, approached the plate.

The left-hander from Georgia also walked, scoring Alou from third, and giving Blomberg his first RBI of the season. It was, of course, history's first RBI by a designated hitter. Alou's brother Felipe followed with a double to score two more runs and though the BoSox would go on to win 15-5, after a half inning the Yankees had a three run lead, American League owners had the offense they wanted, and baseball, unlike Lot's wife, would refuse to look back.

While the most powerful of today's pitchers throw no harder than Bob Feller in the '40s, major league hitters have grown bigger and stronger. Individual owners have replaced the last of the 1970s' cookie cutter ballparks with new stadiums containing not only intimately expensive box seating where foul territory used to squat for free but shorter fences which whisper enticements to anyone holding a bat. Outside it all the Rules Committee abides, ready to step in and take charge, make change if necessary should the lesson of baseball's past somehow be forgotten—offense sells.

3RD

A Pitcher's Timeline

July 15 **George Bradley**, of the St. Louis Brown
1876 Stockings throws the first recorded no-
hitter in National League history. St.
Louis wins the game 2-0 over Hartford.

March 29
1867

June 12
1880

Lee Richmond, of the Worcester Ruby
Legs pitches the first officially
recorded perfect game in major league
history against the Cleveland Blues,
winning 1-0. Five days later John Mont-
gomery Ward of the Providence Grays
will pitch the second official
perfect game, winning 5-0 against
the Buffalo Bisons.

Denton True "Cy" Young,
the oldest pitcher elected to
Baseball's Hall of Fame, is
born in Gilmore, Ohio.

July 21 **Jim "Pud" Galvin** of the St. Louis Browns faces
1892 **Tim Keefe** of the Philadelphia Phillies in a match-up
of 300-game winners. Keefe triumphs 2-0. Not until
1986, when Don Sutton and Phil Niekro duel, will
two 300-game winners meet again.

The distance between pitcher's mound and home plate
moves from fifty feet to sixty feet, six inches. The "pitcher's
box" is replaced by a hard rubber slab, on which pitchers are
required to place their rear foot when beginning the wind-up.

March 7	July 7	August 2
1893	**1900**	**1907**

Kid Nichols of the Boston
Beaneaters becomes the
youngest player, at thirty,
to win 300 games, beating
the Chicago Cubs 11-4. He
will go on to win 361
games in his career.

Nineteen-year-old rookie pitcher **Walter Johnson** debuts for the
Washington Nationals. He gives up his first hit to Ty Cobb of the
Detroit Tigers. Johnson loses the game 3-2 but will amass 417
victories in a twenty-one-year career.

Two Hall of Fame pitchers end their careers on the same day with a final match-up. **Mordecai "Three Finger" Brown** (right) pitches for the Chicago Cubs, while Christy Mathewson takes the mound for the Cincinnati Reds. Both pitchers are past their primes and yield a total of 34 hits. Mathewson and the Reds win 10-8.

September 4
1916

July 3
1912

Rube Marquand of the New York Giants beats the Brooklyn Robins for his 19th consecutive victory, a modern record. He ended the previous season with 2 wins, giving him 21 in a row, also a record.

July 19
1910

Cy Young wins the 500th game of his career, pitching the Cleveland Naps to victory. He would win a total of 511 in his career.

February 9
1920

The rules committee bans the use of all foreign substances on pitched balls, signaling the end of the "spitball" era. Pitchers caught "doctoring" the ball will be suspended for ten days.

Boston Red Sox lefty **Babe Ruth** pitches 13 scoreless innings in a 14-inning victory in the second game of the World Series against the Brooklyn Robins. He will go on to hurl 29 $^2/_3$ scoreless World Series innings.

October 9
1916

October 10
1926

While reputedly nursing a hangover, St. Louis Cardinals pitcher **Grover Cleveland Alexander** appears in relief in the final game of the World Series against the New York Yankees. Having started and won two games in the series already, Alexander comes in to face Tony Lazzeri with the bases loaded and strikes him out. He stymies the Yankees for two more innings to give the Cardinals the championship.

July 10
1934

In what will become one of the most famous feats in baseball history, **Carl Hubbell** of the New York Giants, pitching for the National League in the All-Star game, strikes out five future Hall of Famers in a row: Babe Ruth, Lou Gehrig, Jimmie Foxx, Al Simmons, and Joe Cronin.

The first members of the Hall of Fame are selected. The group of five players includes two pitchers: **Walter Johnson** and **Christy Mathewson**.

January 9
1936

June 15
1938

Cincinnati Red **Johnny Vander Meer** becomes the first, and only, major league pitcher to throw back-to-back no-hitters, whipping the Brooklyn Dodgers 6-0. Four days earlier he had blanked the Boston Bees 3-0.

August 26
1947

Dan Bankhead of the Brooklyn Dodgers becomes the first black pitcher in the major leagues, appearing in relief against the Pittsburgh Pirates. In 3 $\frac{1}{3}$ innings he is shelled for eight runs on ten hits, but he homers in his first major league at-bat.

July 9
1948

Satchel Paige, known as the greatest pitcher in the history of the Negro leagues, makes his major league debut. He pitches two innings in relief for the Cleveland Indians.

September 22
1954

By striking out 15 New York Giants, Brooklyn Dodger **Karl Spooner** sets a record for Ks in a major league debut and wins 3-0. Houston's J.R. Richard will tie the record in 1971. In his next start, four days later, Spooner will strike out 13 Pirates while throwing his second shutout.

October 8
1956
Don Larsen of the New York Yankees pitches the only perfect game in post-season history. The Yankees beat the Brooklyn Dodgers 2-0.

May 26
1959
Pittsburgh Pirate **Harvey Haddix** pitches a perfect game for 12 innings against the Milwaukee Braves but loses 1-0 in the 13th.

July 3
1963
In one of the great match-ups in the history of the game, **Juan Marichal** of the San Francisco Giants pitches 16 innings to defeat  Warren Spahn of the Milwaukee Braves 1-0. Spahn pitches 15 $^1/_3$ innings before surrendering a homerun to Willie Mays in the bottom of the 16th.

July 3
1966
Milwaukee Braves pitcher **Tony Cloninger** hits two
grand slams in one game, the only pitcher—and one
of the few players—to ever accomplish this feat.

April 22
1970
Tom Seaver of the New York Mets sets a major
league record by striking out 10 batters in a row.
In the game against the San Diego Padres,
Seaver strikes out 19 and wins 2-1.

November 13
1968

St. Louis Cardinals pitcher **Bob
Gibson** is voted the National
League's Most Valuable Player,
culminating one of the strongest
years for a pitcher in major league
history. In a season known as The
Year of the Pitcher, Detroit Tiger
Denny McLain wins 30 games and
receives the American League's
MVP award.

January 19
1972

Thirty-six-year-old **Sandy Koufax** becomes the youngest player ever elected to the Hall of Fame.

November 11
1981

Los Angeles Dodger **Fernando Valenzuela** becomes the only pitcher to ever win the Cy Young and Rookie of the Year awards.

July 15
1973

Nolan Ryan throws his second no-hitter in one season. He beats the Detroit Tigers 6-0. Two months earlier, on May 15, he had thrown a no-hitter against the Kansas Royals.

April 27
1983
Nolan Ryan becomes the all-time strikeout leader, passing Walter Johnson. Ryan would go to strike out 5,714 batters in his career.

April 6
1989
Orel Hershiser of the Los Angeles Dodgers surrenders the first run in a record 59 scoreless innings.

October 6
1985
Forty-six-year-old **Phil Niekro** of the New York Yankees blanks the Toronto Blue Jays 8-0 to win his 300th game. He becomes the oldest player to accomplish the feat and also the oldest to throw a shutout.

November 16
1998
Roger Clemens of the New York Yankees becomes the only pitcher to win five Cy Young awards.

April 4
2001

November 12
1995
Greg Maddux of the Atlanta Braves becomes the only pitcher to win four consecutive Cy Young awards.

Hideo Nomo of the Boston Red Sox throws a no-hitter against the Baltimore Orioles, winning 3-0. He becomes only the fourth pitcher in major league history to throw a no-hitter in both leagues, having thrown one in 1996 while with the Los Angeles Dodgers. Cy Young, Jim Bunning, and Nolan Ryan also threw no-hitters in both leagues.

May 18
2004

Randy Johnson of the Arizona Diamondbacks, at the ripe age of 39, pitches a perfect game against the Atlanta Braves, winning 2-0.

June 13
2003

Roger Clemens of the Houston Astros becomes the twenty-first pitcher to win 300 games and the third to strike out 4,000 batters, beating the St. Louis Cardinals 5-2.

4TH

A Day in the Life of a Pitcher—
Andy Pettitte

My buddy Bill Dessoffy is a fish aficionado (try saying that three times fast). He's got a big aquarium in his apartment. He doesn't say so, possibly because it'd be hard to enunciate without sounding trite, but I think the fish relax him.

Which is not to say that he hasn't studied fish, which, to me, doesn't sound all that relaxing. But he's done his reading. He knows his freshwater fish, his saltwater fish, which fish get along with other fish. I only know the difference between a pretty fish and an ugly fish and that I like my catfish fried.

I tell Dessoffy that I think Andy Pettitte looks like a fish. I shove a Pettitte headshot in front of him and demand to know, "What kind of fish does Pettitte look like?"

Dessoffy studies the picture. He doesn't put his chin in his hand, doesn't stroke it thoughtfully like you might envision, say, Sigmund Freud and his white beard just before pronouncing a particularly troublesome diagnosis, but

ANDY PETTITTE

Dessoffy studies on it. His brow wrinkles just the slightest bit.

If you look at Andy Pettitte's 2004 headshot with the Houston Astros, you'll notice that he's not smiling like teammates Bagwell, Biggio, and Berkman. Pettitte's visage does not relate the chin-locked severity exuded by fellow starters Wade Miller and Roy Oswalt. No, Pettitte's eyes look sad. The lines descending from either side of his nose to either side of his mouth bring his expression down as well. If anything, in the first days of a three-year contract that has brought a favorite son home to Texas, Andy Pettitte appears blankly despondent.

Andy Pettitte looks like a fish.

"He looks kind of like a clown fish," Dessoffy says.

"He can't," I say. "Even if he does look like a clown fish, I can't write that Andy Pettitte looks like a clown fish."

Dessoffy looks at the picture again. I'm afraid that might be his final answer.

"Is there another name for a clown fish?" I ask.

"Yeah," he says. "Anemonefish."

I repeat what Dessoffy says. It doesn't go well.

"I can't pronounce it," I say. I try again. I sound like Ernest T. Bass from *The Andy Griffith Show* trying to say "amenities."

"Yeah. That won't work," I say. "If I write 'anemonefish'

then someone might ask me about it and I can't pronounce the damn thing. I'll look like an idiot."

"The fish in *Finding Nemo* was a clown fish," Dessoffy says. As if that helps.

"Absolutely not," I say. "I can't say that Andy Pettitte looks like a clown fish, and I'm damn sure not writing that he looks like the fish in *Finding Nemo*. There's got to be something else."

Dessoffy's brow furrows once more.

"An Oscar," he says. "He looks like an Oscar, but nobody'll know what that is."

"What is it?" I ask.

"It's a freshwater fish," he says. "Oscars are stoic."

I swear it was like a light switch turning on, a bell suddenly ringing. It was like Groucho Marx had come back from the dead to pronounce, "Say the magic word and win fifty dollars."

Stoic.

Stoic.

Stoic.

Man, Andy Pettitte's nothing if not stoic.

Don't get me wrong. Andy Pettitte is a standup guy. The day before his start I approach Andy Pettitte in the Yankee dugout. I tell him what I want to write about. I ask him for twenty minutes of his time the day after his start to kind of rehash the game.

Two days later, the day we're supposed to talk, a member of the Yankees media staff calls me at home. It seems that the media staff had plans for Andy Pettitte that day.

And it seems that Andy Pettitte said something along the lines of, Uh, I'm sorry. I can't. I promised this guy.

Yep, Andy Pettitte is a standup guy, a man of his word. He's a supportive teammate, patient with fans, available to the media.

But whether on the mound or in an interview, Andy Pettitte is just not smiling. He doesn't appear to be enjoying himself. Ever.

"Oscar's are tough," Dessoffy says. "An Oscar will eat the other fish in the tank." As if I needed more convincing.

"Andy Pettitte's an Oscar," I say. "Andy Pettitte is a fish."

On Wednesday morning, September 10, 2003, left-handed starting pitcher Andy Pettitte is still a member of the New York Yankees. He is and has been the most visible Christian on the team since his arrival in 1995.

"First of all," he says, "every morning when I wake up I try to pray. I'll pray for my family and stuff like that."

On days that Pettitte pitches, he offers up an additional prayer.

"I'll pray," Pettitte says, "first of all, that the Lord just keeps me healthy and safe. And then I pray that he'll help me to be able to be strong out there, and to focus and just give it my best effort, and then also that I'll represent myself well. I'm a Christian and I want to represent myself out there on the mound as a Christian man. I don't want to ever do anything out there to take that away from me.

"It's different when I get here to the stadium. Right before I'm in the weight room working out and stuff like that, getting loose for the game, I'll say a prayer just because I want Him to watch over me when I get out there and take that mound. I know it's not a normal movement to throw a baseball."

On that day in September, every abnormal movement Pettitte has made as a professional has been made on behalf of the New York Yankees. He signed with the Yankees organization in 1991, straight out of San Jacinto Junior College. Within four years he was a member of the major league squad. In the eight plus seasons since, Pettitte has not come close to a losing record. In fact, his winning percentage has been in the top ten of American League pitchers four of those eight years. When the 2003 season concludes he will be in the top ten once again.

In his eight seasons with New York, Pettitte has made the American League All-Star team twice and finished in the top five in Cy Young voting three times. In 1996 he led the league in wins, and in 2001 he was selected as the American League Championship Series MVP. The Yankees have garnered four world championships since Pettitte's arrival.

When Andy Pettitte wakes on this Wednesday in September he will have started 272 regular season games as a major league pitcher, and in each one of those starts he has worn the Yankee uniform. And though Andy Pettitte and members of his immediate family may suspect, they do not know that tonight is the first of just four more regular season games he will start for the only major league team he has ever known.

On this game day Pettitte exits his bed at 9:30, a late hour for a man with three young children, but only the oldest, Josh, is in school. The other two are on "baseball time," attending the Yankees games with their mother, Laura, going to bed when their father does, and most often sleeping later. It is Laura who wakes Josh to get him ready for school, and Laura who wakes her husband in their home just north of New York City.

The pitcher eats breakfast, plays with his children, and eats his last meal before game time, a two o'clock lunch of chicken and pasta, before driving south to Yankee Stadium in the Bronx, arriving around 4:15, after most of his teammates are dressed and making preparations for stretching and batting practice.

"I don't like to sit around in the clubhouse and think about the game that much," Pettitte says. "I want to get here and get going with my routine."

Pettitte enters through the stadium kitchen in the basement, speaks with the staff.

"Some people might say that I'm a little superstitious as far as some of the things that I do," he says, "but to me, if I didn't do it I wouldn't think, Oh my gosh, I'm going to lose. To me it's total routine. My whole life, almost everything I do every day, is so routine that it's almost like the movie *Groundhog Day.*"

In the clubhouse Pettitte's gameday routine begins with a complete workover—arms, legs, back—from the team's massage therapist. Then he sits in the hot tub for a

60

few minutes before beginning his stretching program.

If you couldn't tell by looking at his 6'5", 225-pound frame that Pettitte is an athlete, the stretching regimen would tip you off. The man can tie his shoes without bending his knees.

Although Pettitte, like most major league pitchers on the day of a start, is off-limits to press, he does talk to teammates who pass through the training room where he has set up for the afternoon. His catcher for this night, as on most nights he has pitched in the majors, Jorge Posada (called "Georgie" by Pettitte and other teammates) will come into the training room after his turn in the batting cage. While Posada is taped and Pettitte stretches, they'll go through the opposing lineup, hitter by hitter, and discuss how they want to pitch to each man.

The Detroit Tigers come into tonight's game with a four-game losing streak. The team has won just 37 times in 143 games this season, and is furiously struggling to avoid the Major League Baseball record of 120 losses in a season, set by the 1962 New York Mets. Tonight the odds do not favor the young team. No one on the Tigers roster has ever hit a homerun against Pettitte, though his career record against Detroit is only 8 and 7.

Tonight will be Pettitte's thirtieth start of the season. And though last Friday, in a series opener against the Red Sox, Pettitte suffered his second shortest outing of the year (2.1 IP, 9 H, 8 R, 8 ER, 3 BB, 5K) and took the loss, he has won 12 of his last 14 decisions overall, and 13 of his last 16. Despite the loss to Boston, Pettitte's record stands at 17 and

8. When Pettitte entered last week's game his ERA was 4.01. It is now 4.35. But with his 12th win this year (July 23 vs. Baltimore) Pettitte became the first pitcher to record at least 12 victories in each of his first nine major league seasons since Hall of Famer Stan Coveleski did so from 1916-1926. Pettitte's pitched just over 184 innings this season, yielding 203 hits and 43 walks while striking out 159, a mere 8 Ks shy of his career season high.

His 145 career victories as a Yankee put him ninth on the all-time team list, and he enters tonight's game in sixth place on the all-time Yankees strikeout list, just three behind his pitching coach, Mel Stottlemyre. Detroit batters are second in the American League in strikeouts.

At 6:40 Yankee starting catcher Jorge Posada jogs out to the bullpen in left-centerfield. Two minutes later Andy Pettitte, wearing a navy warm-up jacket, and pitching coach Mel Stottlemyre walk up the concrete steps of the Yankee dugout and across the outfield to join him. Pettitte and Stottlemyre arrive at the bullpen gate at 6:44. While Pettitte checks his spikes, Yankee relievers pour onto the outfield grass like commuters exiting work, as if to allow Pettitte his privacy. As the bullpen staff begins stretching in front of the 399 marker, Pettitte begins to soft toss with his catcher behind the outfield wall. The two are about forty feet apart. After a couple of minutes, Pettitte backs closer to the pitcher's mound. He throws a bit harder. He resembles an outfielder retuning fly balls to the infield during batting practice.

Two more minutes go by and Pettitte begins tossing from the rubber on top of the bullpen mound, but his throws are still soft, almost exaggerated by what he is obviously holding back. Two more minutes and Pettitte begins throwing from the stretch position. The pitches, because now they are, in fact, pitches, are harder.

Still, for Pettitte, the bullpen session gives no indication of the mound performance ahead.

"The bullpen means nothing as far as the game, ever," Pettitte says. "That's just warm-up. Because I really, almost, in the bullpen, felt so good that I thought that I was going to have a great game, and I think maybe you let your guard down a little bit. Maybe you're thinking your stuff is good, and then you end up in trouble. So whatever happens in the bullpen is just bullpen as far as I'm concerned. I throw that all out. That's just getting me loose."

Not until he reaches the pitcher's mound does Pettitte begin to decide which pitches are working, which pitches aren't working.

"I worry about everything when I get out on that mound and see where the location is," he says. "Everything's different—the wind, everything out there is different. It's just totally different."

At 6:57 all activity in the stadium comes to a halt as organist Eddie Layton, also in his final season with the Yankees, plays the National Anthem. When the final note subsides, Pettitte returns to the mound, the wind-up, throwing now. Fans in the outfield bleachers can, on occasion, hear the pop of Posada's mitt as he receives Pettitte's pitches.

Pettitte with pitching coach Mel Stottlemyre

At seven o'clock, Posada jogs in from the bullpen. Pettitte once again dons his warm-up jacket, and he and Stottlemyre return across the outfield at a walk, without talking.

"I always ask him if he has anything special he wants to say to me about some of the hitters, or anything like that," Pettitte says. "He didn't really have much to say. On the way back in I just always try to remind myself to stay down. Let's stay down."

Pettitte begins the game

At 7:04 Pettitte and his teammates take the field. As Nick Johnson, the first baseman, tosses the ball around the infield—Alfonso Soriano on second, Derek Jeter at short, and Aaron Boone at third—Pettitte half-digs a hole in front of the first base side of the rubber and begins his warm-up tosses. His first is soft, and lands in the back of the right-handed batter's box before being scooped up by Posada. By his third pitch, Pettitte is in his wind-up. His leg kick gains height. His knee comes to a point in front of his chest. Pettitte takes a deep breath before his eighth and final pitch, the one that Posada throws down to second base.

Andy Pettitte is a fish.

On the pitcher's mound, his lower lip is more pronounced. It appears as if smiling would take a near superhuman effort. It is not that he scowls, but rather willfully drains his face of all expression. What emotion that is communicated is by accident, and can only be picked up in the solid, frequent yet unevenly spaced breaths Pettitte takes that cause his entire upper body to move as he exhales.

"I really feel like that's why I've had some success since I've been up here," Pettitte says. "Ever since I was young, I was always able to control myself whenever situations got tight, and to me all that is relaxing yourself. When you get tight, when pitchers get tense, their ball, they start cutting stuff off.

"For me, when I take a deep breath and blow it out, it

relaxes everything. And then, I don't want anything to phase me. If I let them know that I'm rattled over there, that gives them a little bit of an edge, and I don't want anybody to ever have an edge on me mentally."

His head is tilted forward at an angle, downward, despite the mound being raised a mere ten inches above home plate. His glove is held high. His cap is pulled low. Pettitte stares through the determinedly small area to register Posada's sign. Only his eyes are visible to the batter. At times it seems impossible that Pettitte can actually see the catcher's mitt.

"I'm not looking at the catcher," he says. "I'm trying to see the pitch before I even throw it, so I know I pick up the catcher's mitt late, but I try to know exactly where I'm going."

The left-hander brings a five-pitch arsenal to the mound—a two-seam fastball, a four-seam fastball, a curveball, a change-up, and one of the best cutters in the majors. At precisely 7:07, Detroit centerfielder Alex Sanchez steps into the batter's box. Sanchez has not hit a homerun in more than a year. Pettitte pulls his cap down, shrugs his shoulders forward as if impersonating a windmill, nods, and throws a strike. The second pitch is inside. Twice Pettitte shakes off the third pitch, nods, then shakes again. Sanchez is out in front of the off-speed pitch and hits a soft liner to Nick Johnson at first base. The at-bat, for Sanchez, is not atypical. He leads the American League with 34 infield hits. Pettitte comes off the mound to cover first, but Johnson takes it himself, and Sanchez is barely out as he slides headfirst into the bag. Tiger manager Alan Trammel comes out to argue, but the conversation is a short one. Third baseman Danny Klassen steps to the plate.

Although Klassen has played nearly every day for the Tigers since mid-August, he's played in less than 100 major league games since his debut in 1998. He's hit 6 career homeruns, and half of those came in his rookie season. This will be his last major league start for over a year.

Pettitte's first pitch is a fastball, high, but called a strike. Another fastball hits the outside corner to bring the count to 0-2. Pettitte wastes no time. He throws a cutter down and in to the right-hander as Klassen swings and misses for the second out of the game.

With such a young team, there are few Tigers that Pettitte has any real experience facing. But rightfielder Bobby Higginson is the exception, not the rule.

"Dmitri Young and Higginson and Pena," Pettitte says. "Those are the guys that I know, the guys that I had faced before. The other guys, I had never faced them and had no idea, so going through the game you take them all as fast-ball hitters and just see how they're trying to approach you in the first and second at-bats."

Higginson is the longest-tenured and highest-paid player on the Tigers, pulling down nearly twelve million dollars for the 2003 season. But in nearly 40 at-bats against Pettitte he's never taken the pitcher deep and his batting average is less than .220.

Pettitte brings hands up, ready to pitch even before Higginson is set. He delivers an outside strike at the knees to the left-handed batter, who appears to be taking all the way. Once again Posada moves outside, his glove just off the plate.

"Everybody has him set up different," Pettitte says of his catcher. "You know, Mussina is a real, real, real, real good command pitcher, and I think Moose might have him move a little bit more off the plate. Maybe Roger [Clemens] also. I try to rely a little bit more on my movement and stuff like that and try to throw the ball on the plate a little bit more and hopefully sink some stuff and cut it."

Pettitte hits the mitt, but the pitch is called a ball. He throws another fastball, outside again, but this time catching the corner, is swung on and missed for strike two. A cutter, down and away to the left-hander, drifts to even the count. Pettitte comes back with another cutter, and Higginson is tempted, leans over the plate, but doesn't swing. The count is full.

A low fastball on the payoff pitch is grounded sharply back to the mound. Pettitte jumps, gloves the ball, and tosses softly to Johnson at first for the third out of the inning. The pitcher wipes his brow like a yardman in search of lemonade on his walk to the dugout.

Right-hander Gary Knotts is tonight's opposing pitcher. It is just the 16th start of Knotts's career. His first pitch is laced into centerfield by Alfonso Soriano for a single. Nick Johnson walks, and then Derek Jeter, slumping, strikes out. Jason Giambi, in his first season as a Yankee, pops weakly to second for the second out before Bernie

Williams works Knotts for a walk.

With two out and the bases loaded, Posada singles up the middle, scoring two. Hideki Matsui follows with a two-run double that one-hops the rightfield wall for a 4-0 Yankee lead before Detroit second baseman Shane Halter makes a nice grab on an Aaron Boone flare to end the inning.

Pettitte continues to work quickly in the second. He approaches the mound from second base, takes the throw from third baseman Boone, and toes the rubber.

His first pitch to left-hander Dmitri Young is a slow curve on the outside corner for strike one. A fastball inside is fouled into the dirt to bring the count to 0-2. Pettitte's third pitch of the inning gets away and sails high before a cutter in the dirt entices a check swing from Young for Pettitte's second strikeout of the night.

A fastball strike, again on the outside corner to left-fielder Craig Monroe, puts Pettitte ahead in the count again before Monroe grounds an outside change-up hard to Soriano at second for a 4-3 putout.

Pettitte starts the left-handed Carlos Peña with a curveball outside as he did to Dmitri Young. This pitch, however, stays outside. Another off-speed pitch floats low for ball two. Posada sets up low and away and Pettitte misses off the corner to bring the count to 3-0. He doesn't give in. The cripple pitch is a fastball, low and on the outside corner. He follows with another fastball, just as low, but the pitch catches more of the plate and Pena hits it hard into center for the Tigers' first hit of the game.

The number-seven hitter, Shane Halter, is right-hand-ed, but, as with Young and Pena, Pettitte starts him off with a curveball. The pitch stays high for ball one, and the following day Pettitte will admit to feeling "real inconsistent" with the curve. Posada sets up on the outside corner, but the 1-0 pitch sails toward the middle of the plate and Halter pulls the ball to Boone at third for the 5-3 putout and the end of the Tiger second.

Knotts comes out for his half of the inning and quickly gets Karim Garcia to fly out to center and Soriano to pop up to the catcher, but first baseman Nick Johnson pulls an 0-1 pitch down the right field line for a home run.

"Sometimes you get in a jam," Pettitte says, "and all of a sudden you'll get out of rhythm, where in other games, no matter what kind of jam you're in, you feel like you stay in synch the whole time. It's amazing out there. You just have to control your emotions and your adrenaline and everything. Every day you're different out there. And that's what separates the good pitchers from the bad pitchers."

In the top of the third inning, Pettitte gets into a jam.

Catcher Brandon Inge leads off for Detroit. Satisfactory offensive production is a season away. In September 2003 Inge is struggling to stay above the Mendoza Line. He enters the game batting .204 with just eight homeruns on the season.

Pettitte starts him off with a change-up that stays well outside to the right-handed batter. The 1-0 pitch is a fastball

Pettitte hits his mid-game stride

down the pipe, and Inge swings and misses. Pettitte comes back with another outside change-up, but this time Inge can't hold a check swing. The count goes to 1-2. The catcher tops a curveball foul, then pulls a cutter foul in a defensive swing. Pettitte bounces a curve in the dirt before throwing a fastball, low and inside. Inge swings and misses, and the strikeout ties Pettitte with his pitching coach for fifth on the all-time Yankee list.

The Tigers' number-nine hitter is shortstop Ramon Santiago. Santiago is batting .221 with just two homeruns on the season in nearly 400 at-bats. Pettitte starts him off with a curve that stays low. Another curve is low and inside, so Pettitte challenges the hitter with a fastball, but it, too, is low, and all of a sudden he's 3 and 0 to the last man in the Detroit order.

Pettitte throws another fastball, not giving in, but the pitch, according to the umpire, stays low. Pettitte and Posada disagree, but neither speaks. On the mound Pettitte takes a breath heavy enough to move his chest and shoulders.

"I threw two curveballs for a ball to Santiago," Pettitte says, "and then I threw a four-seamer that cut on me big-time, and then I threw a 3-0 fastball right down the middle, and the umpire called it a ball. I guess he called it low. That kind of bothered me because this guy's not going to take me deep. I'm just trying to throw the ball right down the middle."

Santiago has decent speed, but the Tigers are down by four runs, and Andy Pettitte has one of the best pickoff moves in the majors.

Alex Sanchez returns to the plate, and Pettitte works from the stretch. He stands sideways to homeplate, his right arm in a modified chicken wing in order to hold the edge of his glove between his nose and upper lip. With hat pulled low and glove covering most of his face, Andy Pettitte could hold up a convenience store.

Sanchez attempts a drag bunt but misses the low fastball for strike one. A curve low and outside follows to even the count. Sanchez bunts a high curve straight down into the ground, and Posada walks the ball back to Pettitte on the mound. The catcher's face is blocked by his mask.

He speaks, pats Pettitte on the chest. Pettitte, still facing home plate, says, "Okay," more in acknowledgment of Posada's presence than any kind of agreement, and when Posada sets up behind home plate Pettitte throws two cutters in succession, both low, both inside to run the count full.

The payoff pitch is a low fastball, and Pettitte finds himself with runners on first and second after walking two players with fewer than 15 career homeruns between them.

"That really flustered me," he says, "because I felt like I was still feeling okay. I felt like I was in a pretty good rhythm. So really, after I walked Sanchez, I got a little flustered because I couldn't believe it. I'm thinking, What are you doing?

"The main reason is because it's five to nothing and I just walked the number-nine hitter and the number-one hitter, so I'm seriously aggravated at that time. You don't do that. I don't care what happens. You can't walk those guys right there."

Posada takes a step toward the mound and yells out at Pettitte, who nods, then checks the runner at second as Klassen steps into the batter's box. Pettitte starts him off with a pitch low and inside, and the 1-0 count to a batter who looked completely overmatched in his first plate appearance brings out both catcher and pitching coach.

"I don't really know what people come out there and tell me," Pettitte says, "because, to tell you the truth, my head's in what I've got to do, and I'm just nodding and saying, Yeah, whatever. They probably think they're coming out and doing a great job of getting you back in the rhythm or whatever, but I'm already thinking about the next hitter and what I'm doing wrong and stuff like that while they're out there trying to talk to me."

Pettitte does nod, but he keeps his head down, then looks up at the plate. He doesn't face either man.

Umpire Sam Holbrook makes it halfway to the mound before the meeting breaks up. Stottlemyre jogs across the first base line back to the dugout while Posada walks back to the plate with his catcher's mask perched on his head like a pair of Oakleys.

A Pettite fastball, low and in, is fouled back by the right-handed batter. Another fastball comes in on his hands, and Klassen defensively fouls it off his front foot. A third fastball also comes in tight and shatters Klassen's bat. The runners are moving on the pitch.

Klasson is left with only the handle as the barrel flies out toward the pitcher's mound. Pettitte's body adopts a proper fielding position at the same time his head jerks toward third base, as if his head alone is operating on instinct to the flying wood. The ball follows and Pettitte fields it cleanly. Posada stands at home, pointing to first base, but Pettitte turns to second to start the double play. He turns too quickly. Pettitte throws the ball behind second baseman Soriano covering, behind the runner moving from first, and into center field.

"I thought the bat might hit me," Pettitte says. "I could tell it was coming at me, but I was trying to concentrate so hard on catching the ball I was just going to let the bat hit me, and then make the throw. Right when I go to make the throw, I didn't even see the runner going. I didn't know that they were running. Then the next thing I know he's standing on the base and Sory's standing there, and I just made a bad throw."

Santiago scores. Sanchez moves to third and Klassen is safe at first. Detroit has a run in. They have two men on and only one out in the inning. Not only are they hitless for the frame, but they have yet to hit the ball past the pitcher's mound.

The veteran Higginson approaches the plate. Pettitte tosses the ball to first to check Klassen, adjusts his cap, and then challenges the right-fielder—a high rising fastball that Higginson swings through for strike one. Again Pettitte works from the stretch, right arm tucked tight against his body. He takes a heavy breath into the webbing of his glove before coming back with a change-up that Higginson fouls into the dirt.

On the 0-2 Pettitte throws a seemingly good pitch—a change-up low and off the plate outside. Higginson is caught offstride. He's in front of the ball, but somehow manages to flick his bat. The hit is eerily similar to Luis Gonzalez's Game Seven winner over the Yankees in the 2001 World Series. The ball floats gently over Derek Jeter's head and drops into shallow centerfield for the Tigers' first base hit of the inning. Sanchez trots in from third.

"It was a good pitch, there's no doubt," Pettitte says, "but for him to get to it where it was, he shouldn't have been able to get a base hit off of it. I should've made him a little more honest inside.

"In the back of my mind, I wanted to go in. I was kicking myself that I didn't go in after I threw it, because there's no way he should cover that pitch. I should've gone in a pitch before that, because I threw two balls outside on the corner last time he was up, so he'd already seen stuff away. I was kind of kicking myself for not showing him in before I went away right there.

"Stuff like that," Pettitte says, "is what you think about as the game goes on."

The Yankees now lead 5-2, but there's still only one out with runners occupying first and second.

If there is a Detroit Tiger to be feared, his name is Dmitri Young. The switch-hitter is big, powerful. He stands 6'2" and weighs 245 pounds. He will finish the season with 29 home runs, 85 RBIs, and a .297 batting average—not bad numbers on a team that will fight to avoid setting a major league record for losses in a season. Dmitri Young is also unknown. Young spent his first six major league seasons in the National League. Before tonight, Andy Pettitte had never faced him.

Young fouls a first pitch curve toward third. He's late on a high fastball, buts fouls it hard toward first. Pettitte stands perpendicular to the plate before throwing the cutter, low and inside to the right-hander, for career strikeout number 1,258, which passes Mel Stottlemyre on the all-time Yankee strikeout list. The ball is taken out and tossed into the Yankee dugout, where Stottlemyre, briefly, inspects the ball.

Pettitte starts the right-handed Craig Monroe with a fastball on the inside corner. A high fastball, like the second pitch to Young, comes next, but Monroe swings and misses. It's the 11th consecutive strike thrown by Pettitte. The next pitch is bounced in the dirt but blocked nicely by Posada. Pettitte nods from the stretch and throws another high fastball. Monroe fouls the ball straight back. Still 1-2, Pettitte checks first, then second before bouncing another curve. He breathes again, heavily, through his mouth, checks Posada's sign, and nods. Monroe fouls a cutter into the dirt.

Pettitte has now thrown 33 pitches in the inning, and Monroe is hanging tough. A cutter runs low and outside, once again in the dirt, once again blocked by Posada, to bring the count full, and, with two outs, the runners will go on the pitch.

Pettitte places the edge of his glove between his nose and mouth, breathes heavily, and throws outside for ball four. Monroe earns a hard-fought walk, and for a split second Pettitte seems to actually grit his teeth. The usual complacent look, for a second, is replaced by a scowl.

"He battled me," Pettitte says. "There's no doubt. He made me try to make perfect pitches to him.

"I knew a lefty was up next and, for me, I had two outs. I'll get the lefty out if I don't get this guy out. I knew he had a lot of pop, and I was trying to make a perfect pitch to him there because he was battling me so hard."

The approaching lefty is first baseman Carlos Peña, whose single in the second makes him 3 for 8 lifetime against Pettitte. With the bases loaded, Pettitte returns to his windup. He throws a fastball, low and on the outside corner, for strike one before Pena pulls a slow curve right through Nick Johnson's legs at first. Yankees fans are stunned. Two runners score, and Monroe advances to third. The Tigers have batted around. The Yankees' lead has been cut to one run.

The right-handed Shane Halter steps into the batter's box and can't check his swing on a curveball in the dirt. Pettitte follows with two fastballs—low and inside, and farther inside. A third fastball hits the outside corner to bring the count even. Pettitte, back to the stretch, nods to Posada and throws a curve on the outside corner. Pettitte has struck out the side, but also walked three. Four runs, two errors, one base hit, and 42 pitches later, the inning is finally over.

In the bottom of the third, Jason Giambi continues his hitless streak by taking a called third strike. Bernie Williams goes down swinging. Posada singles but is thrown out by Inge trying to advance on a passed ball. Yankees lead 5-4 after three innings.

Inge leads off the Tiger fourth and Pettitte starts with yet another first-pitch curve which, in hindsight at least, is surprising.

"My curveball," Pettitte says the following day, "I felt like I was real inconsistent with it. My cutter was pretty good, but for the most part it was just my four-seam fastball. I was able to throw that pretty much on both sides of the plate after the third inning. The third inning I got in trouble with my command, but after that I was able to move my ball around, which helped me out a lot."

Pettitte goes outside for a ball, a high change-up for a strike, another outside fastball for a ball. Pettitte's third fastball outside is finally swung on and fouled back, and on the second 2-2 pitch Pettitte goes back to the curve. Inge hits it sharply to Nick Johnson, who backhands the ball for the first out.

The number-nine hitter, Ramon Santiago, follows. It was Santiago's walk, followed by a walk to Alex Sanchez in the previous inning, that started the Tiger rally, but Pettitte pleads ignorance.

"Whenever they came up," he says, "I really didn't even pay attention to that. Again, at that time I've cleared my head and I'm worrying about seeing the pitch and trying to throw quality pitches."

Pettitte goes right at him—a first-pitch fastball strike, an outside curve for strike two. The 0-2 pitch is just off the plate, and Santiago fouls the 1-2 pitch off toward first base. Another fastball is popped up by the shortstop and, in foul territory, first baseman Nick Johnson records his second out of the inning.

Pettitte goes after Sanchez as well, but this first pitch fastball is grounded back up the middle for a solid single and the Tigers' best base-stealing threat (he's third in the American League) is on at first.

From the stretch Pettitte eyes the runner, then throws to first.

Klassen fouls a first pitch curve off his left calf. He's late on a high fastball and fouls the pitch into the seats behind first base. Posada looks into the dugout before signaling Pettitte. The pitch-out is on, but Sanchez isn't going.

It's a strange call for sure as Klassen is in the hole 0-2. He can't catch up with Pettitte's fastball, and has looked completely overmatched in all three at-bats. But Pettitte doesn't have the option of brushing off the pitch-out sign.

"That's just Mel," he says. "They're taking a shot, thinking he's going to run. They're thinking they're going to try to run right here because I've got this guy buried, and they want to lead off the next inning with him, so go ahead and try to run the guy."

Pettitte continues to eye Sanchez at first, but he goes to the plate, and Klassen fouls off another fastball to keep the count at 0-2. Sanchez is laughing at the futility of his situation. Try as he might he can't read Pettitte's motion. A cutter low and in to the right-hander stays inside for a ball, and on the 1-2 pitch again fouls off a high fastball. Another cutter comes in low and in the dirt. In this at-bat it's the pitch farthest from the strike zone, but Klassen swings and misses for Pettitte's sixth strikeout of the game. In four innings he's thrown 85 pitches—12 in the first, 13 in the second, 18 in the fourth, and 42 in the troublesome third.

The Yankees break the game open in the bottom of the fourth inning. Hideki Matsui leads off with an opposite field homerun on a 3-1 pitch. Aaron Boone singles to left, and first baseman Carlos Peña commits a two-base error, one of three errors he'll commit in the game and one of six committed by first basemen on the evening, to put runners on second and third with no one out.

Soriano strikes out on a high fastball, then Johnson walks to load the bases. Derek Jeter drives the first pitch he sees into right field for an RBI single. Alan Trammel brings in the 6'7" left-hander Eric Eckenstahler to pitch to Giambi, but that doesn't work out either. Eckenstahler hits him with a pitch, so Trammel replaces him with Chris Spurling, who immediately walks in a run.

In long innings when the Yankees are at bat, Pettitte tries to stay loose. He walks the clubhouse tunnel, sometimes watching part of the game on television in the locker room. Most likely he makes the trip more than once this half-inning.

Posada hits an RBI groundout to first before Matsui strikes out looking on a 3-2 pitch low and away, but the Yankees have scored five runs in the inning and now lead the Tigers 10-4.

On the mound to start the fifth, Pettitte gets two strikes on Bobby Higginson with an outside fastball and an inside curve. A fastball inside and a cutter out are both called balls before Pettitte goes back outside and gets Higginson to swing and miss for his seventh strikeout of the game. Dmitri Young grounds out on an 0-1 fastball. After Pettitte is low to Monroe with a first-pitch curve, the left fielder lofts a high pop down the first base line. Unfortunately, some curse has been placed on each of tonight's first basemen, and Nick Johnson drops the fly looking nothing so much as a young dog chasing its tail. With new life, Monroe works the count to 2-2 before sending an inside fastball back to the box hard. But Pettitte fields cleanly for the 1-3 put out and his first 1-2-3 inning since the first.

Pettitte will pitch one more inning. A groundout, another error by Nick Johnson, then Brandon Inge hits into a double play. Although Pettitte has been strong in every inning but the third, he's thrown 106 pitches through six. The best team in the American League will go on to a 15-5 victory over the worst team in the American League. The only question at this point is whether Nick Johnson or Carlos Peña will be the first to attempt to burn all copies of the game film.

At 10:28 on this evening, ten minutes after Alex Sanchez grounds to Soriano for the final out of the game, the media are allowed into the clubhouse. Pettitte is already showered. He sits in the trainer's room, off-limits to the press, as the media gather in a tight, unorganized cluster in front of his locker. TV cameras work their way to the front and microphones with radio station call letters shoot up as Pettitte negotiates through the crowd to be backed into his locker by the fifteen or so reporters that surround him.

The reporter from the YES Network, which holds the Yankees' television rights, asks questions first—"What about the third? What happened in the third inning?"— and Pettitte talks about having command, losing command, regaining command.

"How does it feel to pass Mel on the strikeout list?"

someone asks, and Pettitte responds with a respectfully humble reply. He's won his 18th game of the season, on his way to 21. Only one American League pitcher, Cy Young winner Roy Halladay, will win more.

The playoffs are a foregone conclusion, a victory over the Tigers expected. The reporters go through their motions. Pettitte goes through his. The air conditioning hums, and whether from fighting a cold, a change in temperature, or being surrounded by a needy throng with notebooks and tape recorders, Andy Pettitte sounds like he's underwater.

5TH

The Craft of Pitching

Before the Pros

I was from a really small town. I didn't know anything about the minor leagues, and all these people were saying, You should be a high draft pick. I had people coming to my house telling me all these things, giving me advice, and they all said, If you tell them you're going to go to school no matter what you'll go higher in the draft and you'll get more money. Well, that sounded simple, so teams would call and say, What's it going to take to draft you? I told them some exorbitant amount of money and said I was going to go to college no matter what, thinking the whole time this is going to make a lot of sense.

On the day of the draft I had a few teams call me and say, If we take you as the sandwich pick in the first round, will you sign? What's it going to take? If we take you in the second round, will you sign? What's it going to take? I said, It's going to take this much money, otherwise I'm going to college where I can put on some weight and learn how to pitch and that's the deal. The next thing I know I'm picked in the eighth round. My plan didn't work out. I really thought that I was going to go to college. I thought everybody in the minor leagues was 6'5", 245, and hitting bombs. So I was a little bit nervous. I didn't know what to expect. Here I was 6'5", 175 pounds. I needed to mature and get some weight on.

— Jason Schmidt

My sophomore year Grand Bay had the best team in Mobile/Baldwin County, and we're in their same area having to come in second in that division just to get in the playoffs. But then my senior year we had some incredible athletes. Seven of our nine guys signed to play Division I baseball, and I think that's pretty incredible. We had some guys like myself who should've gone to some of those public schools but went the better education route. We had a real nice sports venue there at St. Paul's, and that's a big thing. Over the four-year span I pitched I was, I think, 41 and 1.

— Jake Peavy

I didn't pitch that much in high school really. I wasn't the number one [starter] until I was a senior. I was a hitter in high school. I was going to get drafted as a hitter until I came out my senior year and threw ninety-seven. My junior year I pitched, and I wasn't up near that. But then in my junior off-season going into my senior year, I did a lot of weightlifting, benching, and came out my first preseason game and threw ninety-seven, and the next thing you know the scouts are all over me.

— TJ Tucker

I didn't play any organized ball until I was fourteen years old. Where I grew up in western Pennsylvania there was no Little League, no Babe Ruth League, no American Legion, no high school ball. But my dad played semi-pro ball for years in western Pennsylvania, and he started taking me along, and I started playing when I was fourteen in the men's semi-pro league. I played first base.

I pitched a little bit in semi-pro when they ran out of pitchers, and when I signed with the White Sox they sent me out to Holdrege [Nebraska]. J.C. Martin was out there playing first base, and he got a bonus, so I was playing right field and hitting good. I was hitting .340 something. Then all the guys there hurt their arms, so the manager said, Can you pitch? I said, No, I can throw. I can't pitch. So he had me pitch. All I had was a fastball, but I never got back to any place but pitching.

– *Gary Peters*

I pitched a lot through Little League and pitched through high school. I didn't pitch a whole lot in high school until my senior year. I played shortstop up until then. And when I wasn't pitching I was playing shortstop. You know, in high school you only play twenty-seven games, and I think I pitched in something like twelve of them. I would've rather played shortstop. I could throw with all the major league shortstops. I just couldn't run or move with them. I wish I could've been an everyday player, but I just don't think I was given the ability, the athleticism, to do that.

– *Pat Hentgen*

My senior year [in high school] I lost two games. I won nine. Those two games I lost were because of my bad decisions—hanging pitches and giving up home runs. But I was pretty dominant. I had 90-something innings with 125 strikeouts. They couldn't hit my fastball. I mean, nobody could touch it.

— Jerome Williams

I was a walk-on at USC, had an academic scholarship. I wasn't scouted at all, even out of high school. I had hurt my knee and was in a cast my senior year, and never really got a sniff as far as being scouted to play pro ball out of high school because I did not impress. I was exactly what they never look for. They look at somebody like me and say, This guy can't throw hard. He'll never make it to the big leagues.

— Bill Lee

We made it clear that if we didn't go real high in the draft then we were probably going to go to college. A couple of teams showed some interest early, but we said, It's going to take a pretty good chunk of change, and some promise that we're going to move through your system, to go. And I didn't really want to leave home. But the Padres called and said, We just took you in the fifteenth round. We want to talk to you. I laughed and went to the beach. I had absolutely no interest. I said, Listen, I'm going to college. We'll talk in three years when I'm eligible.

A scout comes in three or four times, we finally get some things ironed out, they give me quite a bit of money.

They give me the money as compensation for the round that I thought we should go in, which is around the third or fourth round, so that was nice of them, showed that they wanted to sign me and showed that they were going to invest some money and effort and time into me.

Coming out of high school I was six foot, a buck seventy. It was a gamble. But Mark Wassinger, the scout who drafted me, believed in me, and that means a lot. This guy said, Listen, you can get it done. And you look at these guys who are king of the mountain, they're not the biggest guys in the world. Look at some of your Hall of Famers. You've got Greg Maddux, Tommy Glavine. These guys aren't big, but they're getting it done. I think a lot of times the draft is a bit skewed with projectability.

– Jake Peavy

Conditioning

I didn't stretch at a younger age as much as I do now. I didn't need to. For one, at a younger age, you're a little bit looser than you are when you get older, and two, I was always working out doing low reps. I was lifting really heavy weight with low reps, so it wasn't like bodybuilders who get really big and really muscular. They do a medium weight with a lot more reps, and it gets more of a pump. I was just out for max strength, so I never really got tight. I never got big. I never got stretch marks like a lot of my friends did when they started lifting weights.

– Bronson Arroyo

I never really lift weights (for my legs). The only thing was before my baseball season I had basketball season, so I used my spring shoes. At that time I really wanted to play basketball, because I was a sophomore starting, and I wanted to get my jumping ability high, so I was using spring shoes a lot, and that pretty much helped me with my legs.

– Jerome Williams

I grew up in a strength and conditioning program, and that's always been a big part of my preparation, so I do legs and upper body most of the year. I feel much more prepared when I go out there if I have been conditioning myself for my outings.

– Kip Wells

I think it's good to work out your legs and your stomach. I don't think it's real good to work out with heavy weights with your upper body. Some light weights with upper body is good, but, it's kind of different strokes for different folks. Randy Wolf does a lot more than I do. Everybody here does more than I do, but that's the thing—different people do different things. Tom Glavine worked out a lot when I was in Atlanta, and Greg Maddux didn't work out hardly at all, and they're both pretty good.

– Kevin Millwood

We never did weight training. If we did any weights it would be flyweights. I go in the clubhouse now, and there are weight sets in there, and these guys are pressing big numbers. Even pitchers. And I don't think that's good for them. Lengthening your muscles for pitching, that kind of exercise is better for you. They may throw harder, but I don't think their control is as good now, and I don't think they have as much stamina. They're probably stronger. But there aren't many guys that are good control pitchers. Maybe eight or ten of them.

— *Gary Peters*

Starters vs. Relievers

It's almost like two different positions. I don't know what it is. I can't put a finger on it. I think relievers are a little crazier and, starters, we've got so much time on our hands in between starts we've got a lot of time to think about things and analyze things. Relievers, they can be in the game in any given moment, so they've got to be on their toes all the time, kind of amped up, ready to go, where starters are a little more laid back.

— *Jason Schmidt*

A lot of relievers are a little quirky and, you know, got a funny personality. Most of the starters are, I guess, more analytical and seem to be more studious. The biggest thing about pitchers is that everybody's different. I mean, even if you throw similar pitches at similar speeds as another guy you're still probably going to get guys out differently, and I think that's the beauty of pitching. You can watch how another guy does, but you've still got to figure out how you're going to do it.

— *Kevin Millwood*

As far as a starting pitcher versus a reliever, it's going to depend on which guy has got two or three pitches and which guy's just a one-pitch pitcher. Like Mariano [Rivera] would not be a good starter because he doesn't have that third pitch, or even a second pitch. A guy like Jeff Weaver could pitch with two pitches as a starter because he's got such movement on his fastball, but in general the difference between a starter and a reliever is a starter will have that third pitch, because the third time through the batting order you want to have a couple of different options to attack the hitter with, whereas a reliever, if you're out there for one inning, you're really more of a thrower than a pitcher. You have that one speciality pitch. For Mariano it's the cutter.

– Jim Kaat

It used to be there were ex-starters down there [in the bullpen], so they were starters too. But now you've got guys that are just bred to be relievers, and so they actually carry that persona, thinking that's how they have to act to be a stopper. They used to ask me, How come you don't have a beard? I said, This is the way I look. There's nothing I can do about it. I'm not going to fake it. But I know a lot of guys that grew beards and hid behind that persona a little bit thinking that they had to carry a certain odor about them to do the job.

– Dave Righetti

92

Other Pitchers

Every pitcher is so different. You've got some starters that are just extremely wacky, then you've got other guys, like Greg Maddux, who are very studious, who really educate themselves in the game. As a starting pitcher you have to educate yourself more, about the hitters. You have to be more of a scout, instead of just going out there and throwing. He [Maddux] can see things in hitters that other people can't. He would tell me stuff that just went right over my head, but five years later I'd be on the mound, and I'd see something and think, Wait a minute. That's what he was talking about five years ago. All of a sudden it makes sense.

— Jason Schmidt

I grew up in Houston so Nolan Ryan was the man back then.

— Kip Wells

My two idols are Nolan Ryan and Roger Clemens. I like how they go out and go about their business. Ryan played forever. He just was high intensity. He did his stuff, went about his business, took care of it. He took care of his body. That's the biggest thing about pitching—you have to take care of your body. You can go out there and throw and throw and throw, but if you don't take care of your body, you're never going to make it past ten years.

— TJ Tucker

Randy Johnson–there's a guy that was let go from the Expos because he couldn't throw strikes. Sandy Koufax was another one. They all matured late, and they hung on and became superstars at their position because they eventually learned to throw strikes and learned how to pitch a little bit instead of being throwers. A guy like Marichal, who threw three-quarters his whole life and threw sidearm, and it wasn't until he got in the big leagues that they decided to make him throw over the top, and then he became a superstar.

There are a lot of changing, defining moments in a pitcher's career, and it comes with tinkering. [Tim] Wakefield didn't make it as anything other than a knuckleballer. Hoyt Wilhelm, the same thing. Once they develop a knuckleball then all of a sudden they're a gimmick pitcher, but they make it because they're able to throw the ball over and they're smart. They know when to throw a strike and how to throw the knuckleball, and they succeed because they're good pitchers.

– *Bill Lee*

Baseball wants more offense, so they keep doing more and more to make it tougher for pitchers. There's no question in my mind it was easier for me to pitch in the sixties than it was for Roger Clemens in the nineties. And granted he's got better stuff, he throws harder than I did, but it's just more of a hitter's game.

– *Jim Kaat*

94

Pitch Selection

I'm a sinkerball pitcher. I can always hit that outside corner to a lefty, but it's tougher for me to hit that inside corner to a lefty, so with me standing over farther on the first base side it enables me to be able to get the ball over there on that side easier.

It's almost like throwing a dart. You don't stand over here and throw a dart this way; you line up right here and throw it that way. That's the toughest pitch for me sometimes. It's pretty much tough for everybody, but if you can master the outside, down and away pitch to a righty, that's what you want because most of the hitters are righties.

I win games by being able to hit that corner down and away. That's probably the main pitch I'm going to throw is the fastball down and away to righties. Everything else comes off of that because you can't all of a sudden go over here on the rubber to throw this kind of pitch. They're going to pick that up, of course, so you have to learn which is the best spot for you on the mound, and then you have everything else come off that.

You've got to remember there's another pitcher on the other team that's doing something to that mound, too, so it's kind of tough to be adjusting pitch to pitch because there's different holes in the mound. Maybe there's a lefty pitcher pitching against us that day, and he is completely on the other side of the rubber. He might land in a different spot—maybe near where I land but off just a little bit—so you have to go out there and manicure the

mound before every inning. Dig in there, fill it in there. Whatever you have to do to try to make it comfortable.
— *Dustin Hermanson*

I didn't have what I'd call a cutter. I had a controlled breaking ball. Johnny Sain would get us up there about fifty feet and we'd learn how to make it break a little, make it break a little more, make it break a lot, so you'd have one basic delivery, and you might have three, four pitches off that.
- *Jim Kaat*

I'm a groundball pitcher, and my strength is getting groundballs. I need to work on trying to throw fewer pitches, to be able to work further in the game. That's something I need to work on. For me, the best part of my game is throwing that sinker on the right side. The change-up and the breaking ball needs to be worked on, and throwing to the left side of the plate a little bit more, but I've always been throwing to the right side of the plate, so that's something that I got to stick with.
— *Zach Day*

I'm throwing a fastball, and then I'm throwing a two-seam fastball that's a sinker. I'm throwing a changeup. I'm throwing a curveball at the high slot, and then I'm dropping down a little and making it really sweepy, which looks more like a slider, and then I'm throwing a cutter, a cut fastball in on lefties. Like Mariano Rivera, what he throws.

Hitters, a lot of times, are only going to react to what

they see at the plate. And there are a lot of different things going on out there that are hard for me to explain. For instance, last game when I pitched here against the Yankees, I threw three pitches to Jason Varitek. Alex Rodriguez, second at-bat. Varitek calls a fastball away. In the middle of my wind-up something told me, This guy's geared up for a fastball. Do not throw him a fastball. So I'm throwing him a fastball away, but I just took a lot off of it, and it went about eighty miles an hour. He swung through it and missed it, and Varitek knew what I was doing because he sees me do it all the time. But the guys upstairs probably said, Ooh, he just threw him a first-pitch change-up, when actually I threw a fastball down, but I just took a little bit off of it because I had a feeling that he was geared up for a fastball.

I feel like I go a little bit more on gut than a lot of other people do. I feel like, in my career, that's gotten me to where I'm at, kind of picking hitters by seeing what's going on during the game. But initially, if you don't know the guy, we're going probably 90 percent by the book, but as you get a feel for them and they get a feel for you and you see how they react to your pitches, you start creeping a little bit closer towards more gut.

— *Bronson Arroyo*

Every ball handles differently, and that's the biggest thing I have against major league baseball today—they throw out balls way too often. If it just looks cross-eyed then the hitter gets it or the umpire or the outfielder. I've never seen a more benevolent group of guys throwing away perfectly good baseballs. That's my big pet peeve right now. I hate that. If a ball's scuffed up in three different spots, it's going to actually have more drag. It's going to slow down, but for me, a breaking-ball pitcher, I like it roughed up as much as possible because I could get more rotation on the ball.

– Bill Lee

I throw a fastball and curveball. I didn't start throwing a slider until my junior year in college. It was more of a cutter, but it turned into a slider. My change-up has always been a work-in-progress. It's actually as good now as it's ever been. But, at the same time, when you've got the bases loaded and no outs, or you've got a guy in scoring position with two outs, you don't want to get beat with your fourth-best pitch. You want to stick with your bread and butter, so I throw it mainly to lefties. I use it when I can. The more I throw it the better I get at it, so with that in mind I throw it when I can, but I don't want to get behind in the count because I'm working on throwing my change-up.

- Kip Wells

When I was starting it was fastball, change-up, slider, curveball. I've been throwing the same change-up since I was eight or nine.

- Chris Hammond

The first pitch I learned to throw after the fastball was a slider. Of course, a curveball, but mainly I was a sinker/slider pitcher. The sinker was a fastball, but then later when I got in higher ball I learned how to throw a runner, which is another kind of fastball.

A curve and slider don't go along real good together. You're going to have one good and one just okay. And that's the way I was. I learned the curveball, but my curveball was always slow, just an okay pitch, not a great pitch. My slider was my good breaking ball. Everything I threw was two-seam, but you just released it a little differently to make it sail in on a right-hander as left-handed pitcher, because my other pitch sunk and tailed away. If you didn't have something inside they'd crowd the plate.

– Gary Peters

Being a Starter

If you have a bad outing you want to get back out there and pitch again and make things right instead of waiting five days. If you have a good outing, you want to go out there and do it again before you forget what was going on. I hate waiting five days in between, but at the same time I need every last minute of it to get the arm recovery and the body recovery.

If I was a reliever, it'd be fun to be out there every night, but there's nothing like being a starter because you can keep the relievers out of the game if you're going good. You can pitch the whole nine innings. Everybody wants to be a starter, I think, ultimately.

– Jason Schmidt

For me it's having the preparation, the four days before-hand, knowing when I'm going to pitch. It's knowing I'm coming to the park today, and I need to be 100 percent and the other four days I don't have to gear up.

– Bronson Arroyo

There's definitely a downside. I mean, if you go out there and have a rough game you have to wait four days—four more days in between—to go out there and redeem yourself, whereas in relieving you can have a rough game tonight, and you can go out tomorrow night and be the hero.

I did both. I was a closer. I've been a long relief guy, a set-up guy, a mop-up guy all the way to a starter and a closer. I did them all, and it's tough to adjust right away. You pretty much have to train yourself for what you're doing. That's why you hear a lot of guys say, He's adjusting. A lot of times you'll see maybe a starter go to the bullpen, and it'll take him awhile to get adjusted to it, just as a bullpen guy going into the starting rotation. It's a big adjustment.

The best part about starting is you know when you're going to pitch. You can get on a good schedule, a good routine of when to work out, when to lift, when to run, when to take your bullpen. You know exactly what's going to happen. Being a reliever you have to be ready every day. It's a different routine. You have to work in your workouts whenever you can. I don't know how those guys do it all the time. It's tough. As a starter you have to go out there and have endurance. Most relievers, unless you're a long relief guy, go out there and most of the time pitch an inning, maybe a little more, maybe just to one hitter, so that's more of a sprint whereas a starting pitcher's an endurance kind of person.

To me it's a completely different position almost. It's almost a completely different job. But one thing about it is the same—you have to get guys out. No matter what you do, pitch starting or relieving, your job is just to get guys out at the plate.

– *Dustin Hermanson*

I think being a starting pitcher in this league is the best gig going. To go from playing thirty-four or thirty-five times a year to playing 150 to 162 times doesn't make a whole lot of sense to me.

– *Kevin Millwood*

You have a workout program. The day after you pitch you can lift as much as you want—legs, upper body. The next day you go out there and throw on the side. You do your lower body the day after you pitch and your upper body the next day. And you can run thirty or forty-five minutes because you're not going to do anything. Being a reliever you can't lift weights before the game.

– *Chris Hammond*

The hardest part about being a starting pitcher is having four days in between. When things are going great, it's all right, but as a reliever if you have a bad outing you know you're going to be out there in a day or two. As a starter you've got four days to think about that. You almost have to forget about it. Once it's over, after the game, you think about it a little bit, but the next morning when you wake up it's got to be out of your mind. It's easier said than done, but it's something that you have to develop and be able to do.

The best thing is being in control from the start, being out on the mound and knowing that you could carry this team. You're out there, and you know it's your game.

– *Zach Day*

The best and worst thing can be the same thing sometimes. Only having to work one out of every five days is not that bad of a gig. To be able to go out there every fifth day and prepare yourself the other four days, knowing that you're coming to the field that day to get your work done and then just relax and watch another ballgame can be nice when you're rolling, but when you're sucking, it sucks.

– *Kip Wells*

6TH

Coaches and Catchers

We already know that pitchers come in all physical shapes and sizes. The emotional range of pitchers is just as wide. To harness that expanse so that the pitcher can be most effective, the pitcher depends on himself, his family, other members of the pitching staff, his catcher, and the pitching coach.

A primary concern of both the catcher and the pitching coach is to obtain the best possible performance from the man on the mound. While the catcher also has to perform offensively, few major league catchers would swap a homerun for getting his pitcher through an extra inning of work. Defensive skill, including managing a pitcher, is a matter of pride.

There is, of course, some overlap in the duties of the pitching coach and catcher, but while the catcher has been a part of the game since its inception, the position of pitching coach, even at the major league level, is, considering the long history of professional baseball, a relatively new development. Sure, every major league team had a pitching coach by the late '50s, but pitchers who reached the big leagues as late as the mid-1960s might've traveled through the minors without ever receiving the benefit of a pitching instructor outside of the odd, short-term winter ball session.

One might believe that, by the time the pitcher is called up to the majors, he should know a thing or two about his craft. So what assistance can a pitching coach offer? Obviously the pitching coach can promote mechanics and help analyze opposing hitters, but the pitching coach, like the catcher, has some psychological responsibility as well. Some pitchers respond to positive reinforcement, others to negative reinforcement. And it's beneficial to know which pitcher responds to which method on any given occasion.

What does a pitcher want from his catcher? Pitchers from the 1960s and '70s, a simpler time at least in memory, seem to ask less.

"I felt good when he called what I was thinking about throwing," Gary Peters says. "That's just working good together, and most of the catchers I dealt with did that."

Peters, who won the American League's Rookie of the Year in 1963 and twice led the league in ERA, didn't sign with the Chicago White Sox as a pitcher. Instead the left-hander played first base—that is until he got to camp and saw J.C. Martin, a White Sox bonus signing, manning the bag at first. Martin would eventually convert to catcher and serve as Peters's primary backstop in Chicago.

"J.C. was probably the best," Peters says. "I like the catcher to be able to catch the ball into the strike zone. Al Lopez's theory was not to give a target. Sit there with your glove hand on your knee. That way you would catch the low ball up, the sinker, instead of swatting it down. I liked catchers who could do that, that wouldn't swat that ball down, because I was trying to throw the ball a couple of inches low anyhow."

Bill "Spaceman" Lee is very specific when asked what he wanted in a catcher.

"A guy that sits back there, has no vocal cords, has an accurate arm, and stops everything in the dirt," he says. "And a guy that doesn't think too much, because it hurts the ballclub."

Lee pitched fourteen major league seasons, ten with Boston and four with Montreal. With the Red Sox his receiver was Hall of Famer Carlton Fisk. With Montreal it was Hall of Famer Gary Carter.

"Fisk and I had a hard time because he was slow, methodical, and I was a fast guy. Carter and I fit like a glove because he and I were like ADD together, and we would work quick."

Active pitchers appear more charitable toward their catchers' contributions.

"First and foremost, you want great communication," says Bronson Arroyo. "Without question. You need a guy back there who's really into the game and wants you to do well and wants to communicate that with you and wants to talk about how to get these hitters out with no ego involved. That's number one."

Arroyo made his major league debut with Pittsburgh in 2000. While he started twenty-nine games for the Pirates over the course of three seasons, it was not until 2004 with Boston that he was a regular member of the starting rotation. In fact, Arroyo made as many starts in 2004 as he did his entire three years in Pittsburgh, so it's not difficult to imagine that he's happy with his current situation, including his catcher, Jason Varitek.

"He does a beautiful job," Arroyo says. "If I shake him off, and he goes through the signs and he disagrees with me, he'll come out and say, 'Let's talk about it. Let's get this right right now.'"

What does Arroyo not want to see in his backstop?

"You don't want a guy back there who thinks he knows everything and says, You're throwing a curveball to Alex Rodriguez in this situation because I've been in the league eight years and you've been here for three," he says.

"Jason's taught me 90 percent of my game over the last year and a half and no doubt about it, he knows, almost all the time, what I want to do to this guy. We just threw a good fastball. He knows I'm setting this guy up for a breaking ball away, and if anything else is different than that, it's a very rare occasion. It might happen three or four times a game where I've got a gut feeling that, you know what, I've never thrown Gary Sheffield a change-up but for some reason I think I can get him out with that pitch, and I'll shake all the way to the change-up and he'll go ahead and throw it down. But usually I'm not shaking him off because he knows what we're trying to do. It's like an intuitive thing because he knows my game. He knows how I pitch, how I'm feeling that day.

"That's basically all you can ask of a man," Arroyo says. "To work together and try to get it right and just help you out while you're out there."

Jason Schmidt has pitched in the majors for ten seasons, but it wasn't until he joined the San Francisco Giants in late 2001 that he became the dominant pitcher he is today. While the Giants missed the playoffs that year, Schmidt went 7-1 with a 3.39 ERA after being acquired from Pittsburgh. In his three-plus seasons with the Giants his ERA has never been more than 3.50, and over that same period he's averaged more than a strikeout an inning.

Schmidt made the National League All-Star team in both 2003 and 2004. In each season he led the league in shutouts and was among the top four pitchers in wins, ERA, complete games, and Cy Young voting.

"I like a catcher that gives me confidence," Schmidt says. "I like a catcher that makes you think that when you're out there you can throw anything you want and get the guy out. Benito Santiago, for example. When I was on a roll, when I got two strikes on a guy, sometimes he wouldn't even give me a sign. He'd just stick his glove up right down the middle of the plate and just smile. When your catcher's doing that you think, I've got good stuff today."

Santiago was Schmidt's regular catcher when he first arrived in San Francisco, as well as during the 2002 and 2003 seasons. In the off-season, unable to get the contract he wanted from the Giants, Santiago signed with Kansas City.

"He just puts so much confidence in you that you felt

like you couldn't be beat," Schmidt says. "Because to get confidence from a guy with a background like he's had, and all the guys that he's caught, if he has faith in you it makes you feel like you're doing something, and it just made it fun to go out there and pitch every time. I never had so much fun pitching in my life."

"It's the experience behind it, knowing that he's caught guys like Roger Clemens, guys that have won Cy Young Awards. So you're thinking, Hey, this guy's setting up down the middle. He's got confidence that I can blow this ball right by the guy. He's not even giving me a sign. I mean, it was fun. He could put down any finger. It may be the wrong thing to put down, but if you've got confidence in your pitch, 99 percent of the time you're going to get the guy out."

Pat Hentgen has pitched fourteen major league seasons. Most have been in Toronto as a member of the Blue Jays. With Toronto, Hentgen was selected to the American League All-Star team in 1993, 1994, and 1997. In 1996 he won the American League's Cy Young Award.

"I like to be able to communicate, not only when I'm on the mound but when I'm in between starts," Hentgen says, "whether it's in the outfield or in the dugout or at the hotel bar. I want him to know when to light my fire and when to tell me my stuff's great. And the catcher needs to be able to do that with all ten of us, not just one, but all ten of us.

"It can help if you have a good catcher that can get the

best out of a pitcher. Because some guys you can just tell with their personalities, you can't get on them. They're going to crumble. And some guys you have to get on to get them fired up to pitch better."

And which catcher sticks out in Hentgen's mind?

"When Charlie O'Brien came over from Atlanta, I was all excited because he was Maddux's personal catcher over there. I thought, What a great opportunity to get to talk to this guy and pick his brain about Maddux. I ended up having a really nice relationship with him. I ended up having the best season of my career, and I think Charlie had a lot to do with that."

So what does a pitcher hope to receive from a pitching coach?

"Sometimes you can see a mechanical flaw, but you just can't quite make the adjustment out on the mound," says Hentgen, "and by the time you make the adjustment it's too late. You're already in the showers."

"So sometimes the pitching coach can say, Hey, you know, what were you thinking about doing here? Maybe you should try to slow your leg down. They can also talk to you about what pitches to throw because at this point in the game, most of us up at this level have really good mechanics. Otherwise they wouldn't be here. So it becomes a matter of who's good at focusing, who's good at spotting the ball, who's good at making adjustments out on the field. A major league pitching coach should be good at doing those things."

* * * * *

Anaheim Angels pitching coach Bud Black signed with Seattle in 1979, and made his major league debut with the Mariners in 1981. It was the start of a fifteen-year major league career that included stops in Kansas City, Cleveland, Toronto, and San Francisco. Black's time in Kansas City included two American League Championship Series in 1984 and '85, with a World's Championship coming in the latter season. He began his tenure as the Angels pitching coach when Mike Scioscia took over as manager prior to the 2000 season.

He believes a pitching coach can help in a number of ways, "from getting to know their mechanics to see if something is out of whack when they go bad, help them set up a game plan on how to attack hitters, pitch selection to the lineup, give advice, talk about it. What I like to do," he says, "for starting pitchers, is to identify a guy's strengths and weaknesses and have that pitcher totally buy in to what his strength is, what his weakness is as a pitcher. And I think that's the foundation of how a pitcher has to pitch. You know, what can the pitcher do? And then from that, then that's how he attacks the hitter. I'm not one where you attack a hitter's weakness if it's the pitcher's weakness."

And what are some examples of pitchers' strengths and weaknesses?

"Let's take a left-handed pitcher," Black says. "Let's say his strength is a sinking fastball down and away to a right-handed hitter, like Tom Glavine. If the pitcher realizes that that's his strength, he's got to perfect that pitch. Just know in his heart that he can execute that pitch with no doubt, and then be able to expand off that, you know, an inch, two inches, three inches off the plate.

"So if that is his strength, it's not going to take too much longer before the hitters know that's a strength. And that's still a tough pitch to hit. Then you've got to realize once the hitter knows that's his strength, they're going to look for that. So then what is the next plan? He's looking for it. And then we see if that pitcher can change speeds off that spot.

"Let's take Glavine again, who's able to do that. Okay, he changes speeds down and away to right-handed hitters. He does it beautifully. Now you've got guys diving out over the plate, covering that side of the plate. Now, even though a fastball in might not be his strength, that's what he's got to continue to work on. Work on the fastball in. So instead of just picking pitches out of the hat—fastball in, fastball down and away, curveball down, slider in—it's important that a pitcher has a foundation to work from. And that's one thing that I try to do with my starting pitchers.

"What makes a great pitcher is his ability to command both sides of the plate."

Counting a one-game appearance in 1973 (he walked two and was charged with a run without retiring a batter), Rockies pitching coach Bob Apodaca played five seasons for the New York Mets before injury cut short his career. Apodaca served as Mets pitching coach from 1996 to 1999 and Brewers pitching coach in 2000 and 2001 before joining Colorado after the 2002 season.

Long-time pitching coach Ray Miller is known for his philosophy of "Work fast, throw strikes, change speeds." Does Apodaca have a quotable belief system?

"I don't know if there is a philosophy per se, because there are so many ingredients to pitching," he says. "There's the physical aspect of the demanding position of pitching. There's the mental aspect of the position. There's the preparation. To say, work fast, work quick, whatever, throw strikes, that's the physical aspect of pitching, so as a philosophy I think that's too general."

"We can get too complicated as far as pitching," he says. "Not everything is fixed by mechanics. There are too many nuances in pitching. Just too many things. Character flaws. Insecurities. Things that only a psychologist could probably come to a conclusion about. There are so many facets of pitching that make a successful pitcher. All successful pitchers have strong character and a strong will to succeed. They're tireless workers. They're always trying to get better. They're not satisfied. They're driven. And I didn't say anything about talent. The most successful pitchers aren't always the most talented pitchers."

Is there a physical type one looks for in a starter?

"That prototypical starting pitcher, first of all, has power," Apodaca says. "It's a loose body. It's looseness of the muscles, not tightness. You have to have strength, but that doesn't mean you have that Adonis body. The strength is in particular areas, the core area, the legs, and in the shoulder/cuff area."

Tom Seaver comes to mind.

"You look at his upper body," Apodaca says. "He was not a tight, tight individual. He was a very strong individual. Very short legs, but very powerful legs. And it wasn't so much the explosion, because really there isn't an explosion as far as hurtling yourself at the hitter. The explosion happens after you land. It's for the force that's generated by that landing that you need strong legs. It's not just catapulting yourself, if you're a right-hander, off your right leg. It's that landing force that you need the strength of legs."

"His delivery was phenomenal," Apodaca says of Seaver.

"Technically very, very strong. He had a very nice, loose flexible shoulder with power. Then all those other ingredients I mentioned. The driven character of him. But as far as the perfect body, you want to see looseness of the arm. You want to see proper arm action, where there's no hitches, no giddyups, no hooking like a Rick Sutcliffe. Where it's just clean out of your hand. Where it's down, back up, and down and through. So arm action, looseness of delivery, where it is poetry, because pitching is timing and rhythm. You see the maximum-effort pitchers, but the ones who stay around forever are the ones who have that great timing and rhythm, eyes constantly staying on the target, and throwing through a target.

"All deliveries aren't the same. But all the good ones, at the moment of truth, when they land, when the front foot lands, they're all very, very similar in position. They might have different arm slots, but they all look very, very similar in their deliveries afterwards. Not before, but afterwards they're all very similar.

And how does one determine the proper arm slot?

"No matter where your arm slot is," Apodaca says, "it is going to be approximately the same distance from your head to your arm. If you think of [Dan] Quisenberry. He threw from way below, but his head was down there. Equal distance. Arm and head."

"You think of Jim Palmer, a guy who came over the top as much as anybody. His arm was here, but his head had to get out of the way for his arm to come to. About the same distance. If you keep your head and eyes level through your delivery, your arm just finds that natural arm slot."

"When somebody's searching for their proper arm slot, I say, Focus on your head and eyes being level. Do you ride a bike with your head tilted? No. Do you drive a car with your head tilted? No. Then why are we doing that with pitching? If you want maximum power then you have to really focus on your body being in a very strong posture. You see heavyweight boxers throw a punch with their head level, and they're throwing through a target. They work on maximum power when their punches are delivered, so they're working on posture. Same thing for pitchers. Posture is critical."

Wayne Rosenthal was a twenty-fourth-round draft pick out of St. John's University in 1986 when he signed with the Texas Rangers. He reached the big leagues in 1991 and pitched 75 innings, all in relief. When Jeff Torborg was fired as manager of the Florida Marlins in May of 2003, Rosenthal was the organization's pitching coordinator.

New manager Jack McKeon brought him up to serve as the Marlins pitching coach, Rosenthal's first major league coaching assignment. By the end of the year he owned his first World Series ring.

"Every pitching coach is different," Rosenthal says. "Nobody's right and nobody's wrong. I'm more laid back. I'm not a boisterous guy. I'm not a yeller. I'm more of a mechanical guy, a positive thinker. I build positive thoughts into their minds. I work with them, not against them. We work together. I don't tell them they have to do this. If it doesn't feel comfortable, I don't expect them to do it. If it feels comfortable, we work with it. I treat every pitcher differently because they have different mentalities, so you've got to find out the insides of each pitcher of how you can approach them. One guy's mechanical. One guy's not. One guy likes to throw bullpens, one guy doesn't.

"Sometimes," he says, "you have to do the opposite of what their mentality dictates. That's what I do as a pitching coach."

For Rosenthal, there's a time and place for the teaching of mechanics, a time and place for working on the pitcher's psychology.

"I don't like thinking about mechanics during a game," he says, "but there are certain times I'll go out to the mound and I'll say something to them—Hey, you've got to sit back, or you've got to do this—because I want them to get through the inning. But in the bullpen we work on positive things. Sometimes it's negative because you're trying to build them up, maybe get them pissed off or something like that, and I'll say, Hey, that was a horseshit pitch. I'll say it was terrible. I'll be honest with them. That's one thing I believe in. If you're honest with them, and tell them what's going on, they respect you more.

"I've clashed with a few of them, but it didn't last for a long time. That's the way I approach things. Everything's positive. I do mechanical stuff in the pen. I want their body in the best position to throw the baseball. Once they get on the mound it's their game. I don't want to be out there saying, You got to throw this pitch or that pitch, but when I go out to the mound I ask them, How do you want to pitch this guy? I want them to tell me what they're going to do. Whether it's right or wrong, as long as they've got a plan then I'm fine with it."

And like Bob Apodaca, Rosenthal insists it's just as easy to work on a side-armer's mechanics as it is to work with a classic over-the-top man.

"Basic mechanics are basic mechanics," he says, "and I believe if you take a side-armer when he releases the ball, and stand him straight up, it's the same as throwing over the top or three quarters. It's the same thing, but your body is in a different position. You still have the same philosophy—there's balance, there's direction. It's basic pitching."

And like Bud Black, Rosenthal believes that the key to a pitcher's success is pure and simple—command.

"There's one big thing that makes a good pitcher," Rosenthal says, "and that's being consistent. If you can command your fastball and locate it where you want, all your other pitches are secondary. You don't have to throw your breaking stuff for a strike because you know you can throw fastballs for strikes. You throw everything off the fastball. If you throw a fastball here and you throw a slider and it goes right there and it moves, he swings at it. And it's a ball. Throw a changeup that looks like a fastball and drops? You're going to get swings and misses."

2005 Pitching Coaches

Anaheim Angels

The 2005 season is **Bud Black**'s sixth as pitching coach for the Anaheim Angels. He joined the club when Mike Scioscia took over as manager prior to the 2000 season. Black is a former college teammate of Tony Gwynn at San Diego State University, and the second Bud Black to pitch in the major leagues. The first pitched in ten games for the Detroit Tigers between 1952 and 1956, finishing with a career record of 2 wins and 3 losses.

Arizona Diamondbacks

Mark Davis joined the Diamondbacks staff in 2003 and is the lone member of the 2004 Diamondbacks staff to retain his original position with new manager Bob Melvin. Davis is a former first-round draft pick of the Phillies in 1979 and made his major league debut the following year. He was a National League All-Star as a member of the Padres in both 1988 and 1989, and in the latter season won not only the Rolaids Relief Award but the National League Cy Young—the fourth reliever to ever win the Cy Young Award in the senior circuit.

Atlanta Braves

A career minor leaguer as a player, **Leo Mazzone**'s current tenure as the Atlanta Braves pitching coach began on June 22, 1990, the day that Bobby Cox replaced Russ Nixon as Atlanta manager. Earlier, Mazzone had briefly served as co-pitching coach in 1985. The mustachioed Mazzone can be seen rocking on the dugout bench nightly during Braves telecasts. His staff in Atlanta finished either first or second in the major leagues in team ERA every year from 1992 to 2002, and Braves pitchers won the National League Cy Young Award six times between 1991 and 1998.

Baltimore Orioles

Baltimore pitching coach **Ray Miller** is another who never reached the majors as a player. But Miller is in his third tour of duty as the Orioles pitching coach (from 1978-1985, when he left to manage the Twins, and again in 1997 before replacing Davey Johnson as Orioles manger). His previous tenure with Baltimore produced two Cy Young Awards for his staff and five different 20-game winners. Miller also served as the Pirates pitching coach under Jim Leyland from 1987-1996. In his two brief stints as a major league manager, once with the Twins (1985-86) and once with the Orioles (1998-99), Miller has a winning percentage of .472.

Boston Red Sox

Dave Wallace was appointed the Red Sox interim pitching coach in 2003 when Tony Cloninger requested a medical leave. Interim was removed from his title for the 2004 season. Wallace made 13 appearances as a major league pitcher for Philadelphia and Toronto, earning a 0-1 record and 7.84 ERA. After his playing career he worked in the Dodgers' front office, as well as serving as the Los Angeles pitching coach from 1995-1997.

Chicago Cubs

Larry Rothschild was the first manager of the Tampa Bay Devil Rays, leading the club for three seasons. In 2005 he begins his fourth season as the pitching coach for the Cubs. He has two World Series rings, one as the bullpen coach of Cincinnati's 1990 team and one as the Marlins pitching coach in 1997. As a player Rothschild made seven relief appearances for the Detroit Tigers in 1981 and 1982. He earned one major league save.

Chicago White Sox

After serving as pitching coach with White Sox affiliates at the Single A, Double A, and Triple A levels, **Don Cooper** was made pitching coach for the major league club on July 22, 2002. In his previous four-plus seasons Cooper served as the organization's minor league pitching coordinator. A seventeenth-round draft pick of the Yankees in 1978, Cooper obtained his first major league win against New York on September 2, 1982, and finished his big league career as a member of the Yankees in 1985. In four seasons at the major league level, Cooper made 44 appearances, including 3 starts, and finished with a record of 1-6 and an ERA of 5.27.

Cincinnati Reds

Don Gullett has the second-longest consecutive tenure among National League pitching coaches (behind Leo Mazzone). He joined the team's major league coaching staff as the bullpen coach prior to the 1993 season and became pitching coach on May 24th of that year. Gullett was a first-round draft pick of the Reds in 1969 and made his major league debut the following year at the tender age of nineteen. As a member of the Reds he appeared in four World Series (1970, 1972, 1975, and 1976), winning world championships on his third and fourth trips. Gullett also pitched in the 1977 World Series as a member of the winning New York Yankees team. Though never selected as an All-Star, Gullett finished in the top ten in Cy Young voting twice, and surpassed 10 wins in six of his nine big league seasons.

Cleveland Indians

Carl Willis served as the pitching coach for the Triple A Buffalo Bisons under manager Eric Wedge for two seasons. When Wedge was promoted to the majors, Willis came along, and he begins his third season as the Indians pitching coach in 2005. He pitched in parts of nine major league seasons, despite not pitching in the big leagues from August 8, 1988, to April 18, 2001. He started 2 games during his 1984 rookie season, but compiled 265 relief appearances. He finished with a career mark of 22 and 16 and was a member of the 1991 World Champions his first season with the Twins.

Colorado Rockies

Bob Apodaca is in his third stint as a major league pitching coach after prior service with the New York Mets and the Milwaukee Brewers. He is the sixth pitching coach in Colorado Rockies history. As a player, Apodaca signed with the Mets in 1971 and spent his entire career in the New York organization. He made his major league debut on September 18, 1973, and pitched his final big league game exactly four years later. In between he pitched in 184 big league games, all but 11 in relief, and compiled an ERA of 2.84.

Detroit Tigers

A career minor leaguer as a player, **Bob Cluck** had already served as the Houston Astros pitching coach from 1990-93 and the Oakland Athletics pitching coach from 1996-98 before signing on with the Tigers in October of 2002. Cluck is the author of several baseball instructional books, including *How to Hit/How to Pitch, Play Better Baseball,* and *Think Better Baseball.*

Florida Marlins

Mark Wiley became the National League's newest pitching coach when he was hired by the Marlins on November 9,

2004, but that doesn't mean the fifty-six-year-old doesn't come with experience. Wiley has served fourteen seasons as the pitching coach of the Baltimore Orioles, Cleveland Indians, and Kansas City Royals. With the Orioles and Indians Wiley worked under manager Mike Hargrove, and many pundits were surprised that Hargrove didn't bring his former pitching coach along after taking over as the manager of the Mariners. Wiley was a second-round draft pick of the Minnesota Twins in 1970 and made his major league debut in 1975. The right-hander pitched in 21 big league games over two separate seasons, and finished with a career ERA of 6.06.

Houston Astros

A career minor leaguer as a pitcher, **Jim Hickey** finally made the majors on July 14, 2004, when he was called up from Houston's Triple A affiliate, the New Orleans Zephyrs, where he served as pitching coach. While with New Orleans, Hickey worked with a number of pitchers on the current Astros staff, including Roy Oswalt and Brad Lidge.

Kansas City Royals

Guy Hansen was the Kansas City Royals pitching coach from 1991-93. He was the Royals bullpen coach from 1996-97, and he hopes that the third time's the charm as he leaves his position with the Richmond Braves to become the Royals pitching coach again for the 2005 season, stepping in as Kansas City's third pitching coach in four months.

Los Angeles Dodgers

Jim Colborn will begin his fifth season as the Dodgers pitching coach in 2005. In 2003, Colborn's staff led the majors with the lowest ERA (3.16). In 2004, the team dropped to fourth (4.01), finishing behind the Cardinals, Cubs, and Braves. As a player, Colborn pitched ten major league seasons, making his debut with the Cubs in 1969 after being signed in 1967. He was named to the American League All-Star team as a member of the Milwaukee Brewers in 1973, his only All-Star selection and the only year he would reach the 20-win plateau. That same season Colborn set a still-standing franchise record by recording $314\frac{1}{3}$ innings pitched. In 1977, as a member of the Kansas City Royals, Colborn pitched a 6-0 no-hitter against Texas, making him one of two current pitching coaches (the other being Giants coach Dave Righetti) to throw a no-hitter in the majors.

Milwaukee Brewers

Ned Yost was hired to manage the Brewers on October 29, 2002. Four days later he hired a man he'd never met, **Mike Maddux,** as his pitching coach. Maddux, the older brother of 300-game winner Greg Maddux, made his major league debut in 1986, not quite three months prior to his younger sibling, and pitched for ten different organizations over his fifteen big league seasons. All but 48 of his 472 appearances came in relief, and he finished his career with a record of 39-37 with an ERA of 4.05.

Minnesota Twins

Rick Anderson was named the Minnesota Twins pitching coach on January 7, 2002, after pitching coach Dick Such was let go following manager Tom Kelly's retirement. Under Anderson, who had previously served as the Twins Triple A pitching coach, the staff ERA quickly dropped from 4.51 to 4.12. Last season the Twins led the league with a staff mark of 4.03, and Johan Santana became the first Minnesota pitcher since Frank Viola to win the Cy Young Award. Anderson, a twenty-fourth-round draft pick by the Mets in 1978, pitched in just 28 major league games but did pick up his only save during New York's 1986 championship season. Just days before the start of the 1987 season, however, he was traded, along with catcher Ed Hearn and pitcher Mauro Gozzo, to Kansas City for David Cone.

New York Mets

After suffering an arm injury as a freshman in college, New York pitching coach **Rick Peterson** never made it past Single A as a player, but he was born into a baseball family (his father Pete Peterson served as general manager of the Pirates in the 1970s) and has coached for more than half of his life. While the pitching coach of the White Sox Double A club in Birmingham, Alabama, Peterson began working closely with Dr. James Andrews's American Sports Medicine Institute in studying the mechanics of the pitching delivery and soon worked his way up to pitching coach of the Oakland Athletics, where he spent seven seasons. In his last two years with the A's, 2002 and 2003, the club led the American League in staff ERA, and starter Barry Zito took home the Cy Young in 2002. Unlike the standard single-season contract for major league coaches, the Mets lured Peterson away from the A's with a three-year deal.

New York Yankees
After an eleven-season pitching career with the New York Yankees, **Mel Stottlemyre** begins his tenth season as Yankees pitching coach. In those previous nine seasons the Yankee staff had finished in the league's top five in team ERA six times. Before rejoining the Yankees, Stottlemyre served as pitching coach for the New York Mets for ten seasons (1984 through 1993) and the Houston Astros for two (1994 and 1995). As a player Stottlemyre was a five-time All-Star, won 20 games in a season three times, and finished with a career ERA of 2.97.

Oakland A's
After three seasons as the A's Double A pitching coach and one year as the A's Triple A pitching coach, **Curt Young** took the reins of the major league staff in 2004, his first as a major league coach, when Rick Peterson was hired away by the Mets. In his first year the A's staff led the American League in complete games and finished second in team ERA. He pitched eleven major league seasons, all but one as an Athletic, and finished with a career record of 69-53.

Philadelphia Phillies
New Philadelphia manager Charlie Manuel brought up

former Scranton-Wilkes-Barre pitching coach **Rich Dubee** to replace Joe Kerrigan for the 2005 season. After spending four years (1998-2001) as the pitching coach of the Florida Marlins, Dubee spent one season as the Phillies Single A pitching coach and two at the Triple A level. Dubee pitched six minor league seasons in the Royals organization.

Pittsburgh Pirates
Spin Williams begins his twenty-seventh season as a member of the Pittsburgh Pirates organization in 2005. After two seasons as a minor league pitcher, Williams spent a transitional 1981 as a Single A player-coach before working as a coach full-time. He has served as a pitching coach at every minor league level and was a bullpen coach for the Pirates before being promoted to pitching coach in November of 2000.

San Diego Padres
A career minor league pitcher, **Darren Balsey** began the 2003 season as pitching coach for the Padres Double A club in Mobile, Alabama. By Memorial Day he was serving as the Padres pitching coach. In his first full season, the Padres' team ERA (4.03) was fifth-best in the National League, while starter Jake Peavy won the individual league ERA crown.

San Francisco Giants
As a player, Giants pitching coach **Dave Righetti** was one of the first pitchers to find success as both a starter and a

reliever. The former first-round draft pick of the Rangers in 1977 was selected American League Rookie of the Year in 1981, a two-time All-Star as well as a two-time Rolaids Relief Man of the Year (1986 and 1987). Righetti is also second in saves on the all-time New York Yankees list as well as second in games pitched on the all-time Yankees list (trailing Mariano Rivera in both categories). Righetti is also one of two current major league pitching coaches to throw a major league no-hitter. He did so against the Red Sox on July 4, 1983. He has been the Giants pitching coach since the 2000 season, and in both 2002 and 2003 the staff ERA was good enough for second in the National League.

Seattle Mariners
Entering his eighteenth season in the Seattle organization and his sixth as Mariners pitching coach, the well-regarded **Bryan Price** will be working under his third manager. He is also the only returning member from Seattle's 2004 coaching staff, as every coach was replaced in the off-season following the firing of Bob Melvin. In his five previous seasons of work, Price's Seattle staff finished in the top five in American League ERA every year but the last, including a first-place ranking in 2001. Price was selected as the Major League Pitching Coach of the Year by *Baseball Weekly* in 2002.

St. Louis Cardinals
Although he has been at the side of manager Tony LaRussa for more than twenty years, former major league catcher **Dave Duncan** (the only current major league pitching

coach who did not play the position) actually got his major league coaching start with the Cleveland Indians in 1978. In 1982 he was hired as the Mariners pitching coach, a position he left the following year to join LaRussa with the White Sox. The pair moved to Oakland in 1986 and later to St. Louis, where they begin their tenth season in 2005. Although Duncan has been associated with several Cy Young Award winners and has coached staffs to league ERA crowns, his most well-known feat as a pitching coach remains the conversion of a seemingly over-the-hill starter, Dennis Eckersley, into one of the most dominant closers in baseball history.

Tampa Bay Devil Rays
Following the departure of Chris Bosio after the 2003 season, Tampa native **Chuck Hernandez** was hired as the fifth pitching coach in the history of the Devil Rays and the umpteenth pitching coach to serve under manager Lou Piniella. In his first season, Hernandez's relatively young staff improved from eleventh to ninth in ERA in the American League. A career minor league pitcher, Hernandez's previous major league experience includes four years as the Angels pitching coach. He is the brother-in-law of former Yankees, Mariners, and White Sox pitching coach Nardi Contreras, as well as the brother-in-law of former major league pitcher Rich Monteleone.

Texas Rangers
As a player, Rangers coach **Orel Hershiser** pitched arguably

one of the best seasons in major league history. In 1988 as a member of the Los Angeles Dodgers, Hershiser was unanimously selected as the National League's Cy Young Award winner. He led the league in shutouts with 8 and in innings pitched with 267, and tied for first in both wins (23) and complete games (15). He set a major league record by pitching 59 consecutive scoreless innings from August 30 to September 28. The streak included five straight shutouts. He was named Most Valuable Player in the National League Championship Series that season as well as in the World Series. In the Dodgers' five-game win over the Athletics, Hershiser won Games 2 and 5 and managed a 1.00 ERA. He was named *Sports Illustrated*'s Sportsman of the Year as well as Major League Player of the Year by *The Sporting News*. Hershiser also won his only Gold Glove Award that season. He was named Rangers pitching coach on June 22, 2002. While in Hershiser's first full season the Rangers staff finished last in the American League in team ERA with a mark of 5.67, the number fell to 4.53 in 2004, good enough for a fifth-place league finish.

Toronto Blue Jays

After being fired by the Marlins in May of 2003 along with his manager, Jeff Torborg, **Brad Arnsberg** landed in Syracuse as the pitching coach of Toronto's Triple A affiliate. Then, following Toronto's dismissal of manager Carlos Tosca and pitching coach Gil Patterson, Arnsberg was invited up for his third stint (he also worked in Montreal) as a major league pitching coach in October of 2004. As a player Arnsberg pitched in 94 games in six big league seasons, finishing with a career record of 9-6 and a 4.26 ERA.

Washington Nationals

After seven seasons as a minor league coach, **Randy St. Claire** was named Montreal Expos pitching coach on December 4, 2002, and begins his third season with the organization in 2005 in Washington. In his first year at the big league level, St. Claire helped his staff to finish sixth in team ERA in the National League. St. Claire signed with Montreal as a player in 1978 and made his major league debut with the Expos in 1984. He pitched in 194 big league games, all in relief, and when he joined the Atlanta Braves in 1991 it marked the first time in franchise history that a father and son had both played for the club. St. Claire's father, Ebba, was a major league catcher from 1951 to 1954.

7TH

Single Game Starters

In the late summer of 2001, while researching the career statistics of my great-uncle Virgil Trucks in the *Pitcher's Register* of the *Baseball Encyclopedia*, I ran across the baseball records of several major league pitchers with extremely brief careers and decided that I wanted to meet and talk with them. I wanted to know about their struggles, their brushes with greatness. I wanted to know if the experience was worthwhile given the brevity of their stay.

I arranged a trip to Alabama, where I was born and where my family still lives, to interview pitchers there. I planned to travel to parts of Tennessee and Georgia, as well. The trip was scheduled for approximately two weeks, and as my departure drew near, I grew a bit anxious. What exactly was I doing? How much time would these men grant me? What stories would they be willing to share?

The Saturday before I was to leave I made a call to Ted Wieand in Slatington, Pennsylvania. Mr. Wieand pitched two innings in relief for the Cincinnati Reds in 1958, and another $4\,^1/_3$ for the Reds in 1960. He agreed to see me the next afternoon.

Mr. Wieand answered the door and invited me inside. On the television the Yankees and the Devil Rays were playing a meaningless final game of the regular season. Mr. Wieand offered me a seat and, being no more sure of himself than I was, asked that his wife, Joan, join us at the dining room table. I asked questions and Mr. Wieand answered. He told me of his first experiences with baseball, his time in the minor leagues, his brief stay in the majors, what it took to get there. At the end I asked him if he had any regrets. That his major league tenure wasn't longer is a given, as it is with all those who are marked in the pages of the *Baseball Encyclopedia* as having abbreviated careers. That he wished his major league career had been longer did not need to be spoken.

"I would've liked to have started two or three games in the majors to see if I could make it," he answered.

That makes sense, of course. Anyone who pays even the slightest attention to human nature knows that we all want one more thing that we actually have done. As I drove back, satisfied that I was on the right course and eager to travel to the South to speak with more short-term major leaguers, a new curiosity began to form. What about those men who made only one big league start?

One might assume that those pitchers who reached the major leagues only to be granted a single start could be grouped alongside Mr. Wieand. Their careers were somehow abbreviated. A week or two on a major league roster. A mere flicker in the course of a lifetime. And, of course, there are plenty of those examples.

In 134 seasons of Major League Baseball, 173 men started one big league game and never made another appearance at the major league level. This number will change. Men who get but one shot in the future will be added, and others will fall off the list when they're granted a second chance.

In 2004, five men—Abe Alvarez, John Maine, Sam Narron, Chris Saenz, and Eduardo Villacis—made their major league debuts as a starting pitcher and finished the season with just that one appearance. Alvarez lasted five innings for Boston on July 22. A day later John Maine made his major league debut, going 3 $2/3$ innings for the Orioles. One week later Sam Narron's dreams came true, though he lasted just 2 $2/3$ as one of seventeen pitchers to start a game for the 2004 Texas Rangers. On May 1, Eduardo Villacis went 3 $1/3$ for the Kansas City Royals, but on April 24 Chris Saenz pitched six innings of shutout ball, allowed only two hits, and got the win for the Milwaukee Brewers against the St. Louis Cardinals. Saenz, the most promising of these five single starters, was filling in for an injured Chris Capuano. The day following his start, Saenz was optioned back to Double A Huntsville. His season was shut down in July because of elbow problems.

But, of course, other situations sometimes dictate a single start within a major league career. Left-handed specialist Paul Assenmacher played 14 major league seasons and pitched in 884 major league games, only one of which (in 1990 for the Chicago Cubs) was a start. George Bamberger is best known as the former manager of the Milwaukee

Brewers (two tenures) and the New York Mets. Bamberger pitched in just 10 major league games, but in his final big league season, 1959, at the age of thirty-five, he got the start for the Baltimore Orioles against the New York Yankees.

Rawly Eastwick, best remembered for garnering 2 wins and a World Series ring while pitching for the Cincinnati Reds in 1975, made his only major league start for the Cardinals in 1977. "The Mad Hungarian" Al Hrabosky—a famed and feared closer for the St. Louis Cardinals, Kansas City Royals, and Atlanta Braves—made a single major league start for the Cardinals in his 1970 rookie season.

The list goes on. Randy Moffitt, brother of tennis great Billie Jean King, a former first-round draft pick in 1970, pitched in more than 500 major league games, his lone start coming for the 1974 San Francisco Giants. All-Star closer Dave Smith pitched in more than 600 major league games over 13 seasons, one of which was a 1982 start for the Houston Astros.

Perhaps the oddest single game start, however, was made by Minnesota Twins utilityman Cesar Tovar. On September 22, 1968, against the Oakland A's, Tover played all nine positions in one game. He began, of course, on the pitcher's mound and struck out Reggie Jackson but walked Danny Cater (who he immediately balked to second) in pitching a scoreless first. The one inning was Tovar's sum total of major league pitching.

There are other names, at least as interesting if not as well known.

Cardell Camper, for example, got his only major league

start as a member of the 1977 Cleveland Indians. Though one would think the gods of symmetry would demand it, Conrad Cardinal did not pitch for St. Louis, but rather the Houston Colt .45s.

Danny Boone, whose given name is Daniel, made his major league debut in 1981 but didn't start his only major league game until 1990. Lafayette Currence started one game for the 1975 Milwaukee Brewers. Darcy Fast started for the 1968 Chicago Cubs in the second game of a double-header. Fast would pitch in eight major league contests. His first start would be his last major league game.

Stover McIlwain made his only major league start for the 1958 Chicago White Sox, a mere six days after his nineteenth birthday. Why someone with the name "Stover" would need a nickname I'm not sure, but Stover McIlwain did. His teammates called him "Smokey."

There were Mexican left-handers before Fernando Valenzuela and Japanese major leaguers before Hideo Nomo. Memo Luna made a start for the 1954 St. Louis Cardinals, though his entire career on the big league mound lasted a mere two-thirds of an inning. Luna yielded 2 runs, 2 hits, and 2 walks in his only major league appearance. Masanori Murakami fared much better. Murakami pitched in a total of 54 games for the San Francisco Giants across 1964 and 1965 and garnered a respectable 3.43 earned run average.

What would these men like Memo and Masanori and Stover say? What insight would Al Hrabosky, Rawly Eastwick, and Dave Smith be able to relate about the singular experience of starting one major league game? Would they be like Ted Wieand and want one more start? Would they, once granted the opportunity, take their one and only entrance into the starting lineup?

Well . . . .

Don Minnick pitched in two games for the Washington Senators in 1957. His only start came at home against Baltimore. It would be the last game of his major league career.

"I think it was either Wednesday or Thursday night before I started on that Saturday," Minnick says. "They had Roy Sievers Night, and they were playing the Boston Red Sox, and it was jam packed in that stadium. In the seventh inning they told me to warm up, so I come in and I pitch to Boston for two innings. I faced Ted Williams. At the time, I believe he was around 14 straight times on base, with either a hit or a walk. And I walked him." Minnick laughs at the memory. "I elongated his record." Nonetheless Minnick escaped his two innings without giving up a run.

"They throw me out to start on Saturday, so I called my parents and everything," he says. "They lived in Virginia where I'm living now, and they came up to see me pitch against Baltimore. In the first inning there was one or two outs with a man on first, and the fellow popped up a foul ball right there at first base, and the first baseman took about two steps into foul territory and was standing there waiting on it coming down and he dropped it. Then the next batter singled to put two men on." What followed was

136

a three-run homer by Baltimore catcher Gus Triandos.

"He hit it into the center field bleachers so I was behind three to nothing," Minnick says. "The rest of the game I did fairly well until the seventh inning. And then they knocked me out."

The first-inning runs were unearned, due to the first baseman's error. Minnick did, in fact, sail along, yielding no more runs until the eighth.

"I was happy in the respect that I did well through the seventh inning," Minnick reflects, "but then I wasn't happy. They were going to take me out for a pinch-hitter at the end of the seven innings but the eighth man hit into a double play, or I would've never gone out for the eighth. That's just part of baseball."

Minnick is seventy-three years old now, yet still relishes his brief opportunity.

"It was just a great experience," he says. "It's something I never will forget. I never have forgotten it all my life."

Ken Mackenzie and Don Rowe got their major league starts for two of the worst teams in history—the 1962 and 1963 New York Mets. The first-year Mets of 1962 won just 40 games out of 160. The 1963 squad managed 51 wins in 162 games. Was his one and only major league start memorable for Ken Mackenzie?

"I'll tell you," he says, "a bigger deal is the start I didn't make. In 1960 I was with the Braves, and I'd been with them for a little over two months. We pulled into St. Louis, and nobody knew who was going to start the game that night. By process of elimination I decided that it was going to be me. Left-handed-hitting ballclub. I was a left-handed pitcher. As we were checking into the hotel near the park in St. Louis, Charlie Dressen, the manager, caught me at the counter and said, Mac, where are your bags? I said, Up in the room. Why? He said, Well, go get them. They need you in Louisville. I said, They need me in Louisville? What for? He said, Well, we need a starting pitcher. You're a relief pitcher. We're bringing up [Don] Nottebart. So I went to Louisville. Nottebart started that game. And you can look this up, I guess; if memory serves me correctly he pitched six or seven innings, gave up seven runs. Ten days later they sent him back to Louisville. I stayed in Louisville and they brought up Chi-Chi Olivo because he was the hot hand in Louisville at that time."

Nottebart's start against the Cardinals was the first of his major league career, and his only start for Milwaukee in 1960. Is Mackenzie bitter?

"If Charlie Dressen had let me start, there was no way St. Louis was going to get seven runs off me," Mackenzie says. "Not ever. It absolutely shifted my whole career. I was a little lefty that could throw strikes, without a trick pitch, and should've been a starting pitcher. Charlie Dressen is really the guy that tagged me as a relief pitcher."

When Mackenzie's start did come, for Casey Stengel's Mets, he also faced the Cardinals. His mound opponent would be a future Hall of Famer.

"It was Stan Musial Night, and it was the second game of a doubleheader," Mackenzie says. "I would warm up, sit down, warm up, sit down because everybody in New York was making a speech for Musial Night, and it took a long time to get going. I lasted an inning and a third, an inning and two-thirds, something like that, against Bob Gibson. We got shut out. We only got shut out six times that year. That was one of the games we got shut out.

"We were all clinging by threads," he says of his team-mates. "There are nineteen on the '62 team that never played in the big leagues again. And I was one of those guys kind of scratching to hang on, and here's another chance. Sort of my first chance."

Don Rowe who, after his playing career was through, became pitching coach for the Milwaukee Brewers, also had hopes that his major league start would occur in a different uniform.

"I was drafted by Pittsburgh, signed by Pittsburgh, and I wanted to play in Pittsburgh," he says. "We had a reunion of all the Pirate guys, and I told Joe Brown, In 1958 or '59 I had good enough stuff I could've helped you. He says, At one time you were the number-one left-handed prospect in our organization. But then we got a guy named Bob Veale, and there just wasn't room enough for you on the club. So I never did get to pitch for Pittsburgh."

Rowe was pulled by Casey Stengel after $4\,^2/_3$ innings. He balked twice and was charged with three runs, but Tracy Stallard, the man who two years earlier yielded Roger Maris's 61st home run, took the loss to end the longest Mets win streak in history at four games.

"He took me out," Rowe says of Stengel, "and Tracy

Stallard came in and Tracy Stallard blew the game."

After the Phillies rally ended, Rowe says, "I went into the clubhouse and there was Tracy, and he was feeling bad enough. He said, I messed up your start. I said, Ah, don't worry about it. There'll be a lot more. So then we got dressed and went downtown. Well, Stengel, after the game, wanted to talk to me, and I'd already left the ballpark. He was madder than hell."

There were, of course, no more starts for Don Rowe in the major leagues.

Dennis Musgraves also pitched for the Mets well before the "Amazin'" 1969 season. His 1965 Mets trail only the original 1962 team for the most losses in franchise history.

But unlike Ken Mackenzie and Don Rowe, who were selected by New York in the 1961 expansion draft, Dennis Musgraves was a homegrown bonus baby. Before making his first major league start Musgraves made four relief appearances without allowing a single run.

"I really don't know," Musgraves says, "what their thinking was on starting me. They could've been short. That could've been it. It could've been a good time to put me in a starting position and see how I was going to react. I don't know for sure. They didn't tell me why, but I was happy to get the start."

Musgraves made his start at Wrigley Field against the Cubs on July 29, 1965. His father and uncle flew up for the game.

"I remember Billy Williams and Ernie Banks and Don

Kessinger and Ron Santo," Musgraves says. "They were my heroes, as far as looking up to them as ballplayers because they had been around awhile. Of course, I was a Cardinal fan. I grew up in the St. Louis area. The Cardinals and the Cubs were rivals, and I got to see them play a lot before I got to play against them. That was really a great experience for me to be able to play against those guys. I was pretty wide-eyed."

Musgraves gave up a single run, the only run he gave up in his major league career. Cubs shortstop Don Kessinger singled. Cubs pitcher Bill Faul attempted to bunt Kessinger to third, but missed three times. Kessinger was running on the two-strike pitch, and Mets catcher Jimmie Schaefer overthrew the infielder covering, so Kessinger moved to third on the error. Then Cubs centerfielder Doug Clemens bunted toward third as the Mets watched the ball die on the baseline. The game was tied at one and remained that way until Ron Santo hit a solo homerun in the bottom of the 12th. Musgraves took a no-decision in his first major league start. It would the last major league game of his career.

"I didn't know that I hurt my arm during the game," he says. "It wasn't until the next day that my elbow swelled up and locked in a ninety-degree position. The bursal sac was swollen, and so we iced it and thought, well, maybe it's just something temporary, you know. Actually the next series we went to Philadelphia or somewhere, and I don't think I said much about it for a while, but I tried to get up and throw after that, and, boy, I just couldn't do it. It was just too painful. I couldn't even get it to the plate.

"I had surgery that fall," he says. "It wasn't evident what

the problem was from x-rays. They thought maybe it was bone chips. They just weren't sure. The doctor, after the operation, wasn't confident that he helped me out. It was sort of an exploratory operation to see if he could tell what was wrong, and he said he cleaned it out and everything, and so I babied it that winter and went to spring training and started easy. When I got up to throw again with any speed, I had the same problem. I'd throw three or four innings and it would swell up again. They did another operation that year, and they carved some of that bone off to give more clearance in that joint."

After a time, the Mets gave up on their bonus baby. Musgraves was traded to the Royals in 1971 and pitched in Omaha before being released in 1972.

"I felt like I got back to where I thought maybe I could pitch in the major leagues," he says. "I went to short relief. Whitey Herzog was instrumental in changing me to short relief, and it worked out real well. I felt like I did a good job."

But a return to the majors wasn't to be.

"To be honest," Musgraves says, "my first chance at the big leagues I had people pushing me. Of course, they had a lot of money invested, and the people that were counting on me were there and were behind me. By the time I got back in condition maybe to have a shot at it, why, those people weren't around anymore. It was new management, and they had players they were counting on, so it made it a lot tougher to break through the barriers. It's very competitive. Everybody would like to have that chance to try it in the big leagues. I got mine, but it just didn't work out."

* * * * *

Jim Miles grew up in Mississippi and played for former Red Sox pitcher Boo Ferriss at Delta State University. When he made the majors he played for another former member of the Red Sox, Ted Williams. Miles's start came on August 13, 1969, for the Washington Senators. He faced the Kansas City Royals, a first-year expansion club.

"I was actually, at that time, a relief pitcher," Miles says. "That's about the time that everything started to be specialized. During my minor league career I was basically a starter, and then after I got called to the big leagues they said, Hey, this guy's got a pretty good sinker and a pretty good slider. Let's see if we can make him into a relief pitcher.

"So we started working it. I went to winter ball a couple, three, four winters and worked on that. I was actually up there as a reliever, but starting pitching sometimes runs into problems, and they have to press somebody into service. I think that's what happened. As I can recall now, I had very little prior time to knowing I was starting that game. Maybe a day or so."

Was the opportunity meaningful?

"It was a big deal for me," Miles says. "It was huge deal for an old country boy from Mississippi to reach one of his lifelong goals, to start a game in the big leagues."

But Miles's favorite memory from his thirteen appearances in the big leagues had already occurred.

"Mickey Mantle was one of my boyhood idols," he says, "and I had spent hours and hours and hours throwing a ball against a concrete pillar. At that time, this was Cardinal country down here, but my favorite team was the Yankees, and I played the World Series by myself throwing a baseball against a concrete pillar, the Cardinals against the Yankees.

"We knew every player in the big leagues at that time, and we could tell what position and all that. I played the Cardinals against the Yankees, but it always came down to Mickey Mantle winning the game. I'd skip the ball against the concrete pillar and make it hit a homerun or something and Mantle would win the game. Then in '68 I got called up, got into the game. We were in Yankee Stadium the first time, and lo and behold I got a couple outs and there stood Number 7.

"Of course, when I saw the pinstripe Number 7 turned around to me, I said, Oh boy, now what you going to do? You spent all these years letting him hit the homeruns to win those make-believe games, and now you got to try to get him. But the good Lord can be so good to you in that game, and I struck him out on three pitches. That's the big- time memory right there. In Yankee Stadium, and there's your boyhood idol. Of course, I know Mickey Mantle struck out 3,300 times in his career, but the only time I got to face him I struck him out. So that is a lasting memory for me."

The Senators were trailing, and Miles, a rookie in 1968, was called in to mop up.

"I threw a real hard sinker, and Mantle probably knew this was his last year. He was chasing Mel Ott or somebody, trying to get to 535 in homeruns or something like that, so he was just really cranking it. He was swinging so hard that he was pulling off the ball, and my sinker ran away from

144

him. I got ahead of him two strikes by throwing the sinker.

"Well, I had a habit of changing my arm position," Miles says, "going right up on top and a little Luis Tiant move, you know, where you turn your back to him and then come right over the top, and when I turned the ball loose, another fastball. I know Mantle's saying, Well, this guy's ahead of me so he's going to waste a couple of pitches. But little did he know that I couldn't hardly spit at that time, so I reared up and came right over the top, and as soon as I released the ball I said, Oh man, he's going to crank that thing. And lo and behold he took it. It surprised and froze him. Here's a rookie on the mound and Mantle in the batter's box. What's the normal thing for an umpire to do? He's going to say, Mr. Mantle will let you know when it's a strike, but he didn't. It was right down belt-high, and he rung him up. I didn't touch the ground all the way to dugout."

Both Fred Lasher and Mel Behney got their sole major league starts in 1970 with contending teams. That's where the similarities end. Lasher signed with the Washington Senators in 1960 and made his major league debut in 1963 with the Twins after the franchise moved to Minnesota.

"My big thing was always to be an outfielder," Lasher says. "I never wanted to be a pitcher. When I signed to play pro ball, I wanted to be an outfielder, but I threw the ball hard and they turned me into a pitcher."

After several seasons back and forth between the majors and the minors, Lasher had his best year in 1968 with the World Champion Tigers. He managed a 5-1 record and 5 saves in 34 appearances and even pitched 2 scoreless innings in Game Four of the World Series, a 10-1 St. Louis blowout.

By 1970, however, the Tigers had fallen to fourth in their division, and Lasher was traded to Cleveland. It was at home with the Indians on July 12, 1970, against the Red Sox that Lasher made his one and only major league start. It lasted just one inning.

"The reason I only pitched an inning," Lasher says, "is because we got in a fight. [Tony] Conigliaro—I had accidentally pitched him inside in Boston—and they thought I was throwing at him. I wasn't throwing at him. They made a big thing out of this in the papers because they were coming back to Cleveland. Well, the first pitch I hit him, but it was accidental. I was a little wild that year. And it wasn't that great a fastball anyway. Tony charges the mound, of course. Gives me a drop kick. Tries to give me a karate kick. Kicks me in the leg and tries to punch me at the same time. George Scott came from somewhere and grabbed my arms and pinned them alongside my body, so I couldn't swing at anything, and the next thing I know I'm laying on the ground and everybody's on top of the pile. You're kind of sucking up dust is what it amounts to.

"The umpire agreed that I wasn't trying to throw at him, that it was an accident, and they asked me if I wanted to continue pitching. I had to go in the clubhouse and get a tetanus shot because he had cut my leg with his shoe, and trying to be macho about the whole thing I said, Sure, I'll go back out and pitch. Well, I didn't have anything. They took me out in the second inning. I think we ended up getting beat something like 10 to 3."

Lasher didn't give up all 10 runs, of course, but Tony Congiliaro's brother Billy and catcher Tom Satriano, in his last major league season, hit back-to-back homerunsto open the Boston second. It was then that Alvin Dark removed Lasher from the game.

"That was a good year to forget, actually," Lasher says. "I think I was 2 and 10 over there, and it was a matter of going sidearm, three-quarter, overhand. My control was erratic as the devil. Finally I walked off the mound on Alvin. It seemed like every time I went into a game something would go wrong. It just got to the point it was so frustrating I couldn't hack it any more."

Unlike Fred Lasher, Mel Behney was very much a rookie when he made his major league debut with the Cincinnati Reds, the team that had signed the left-hander out of Michigan State. Behney had been up with the Reds for about a week when pitching coach Larry Shepard let him know he'd be making a start.

"We went out for batting practice," Behney says, "and Larry Shephard came over to me when I was shagging balls, and he said, You're backing up. If you back up, that means you're pitching the next day. And that was how I was told I was pitching the next day. I called my parents to tell them because my mom—my dad didn't like to fly so he didn't come—wanted to come and see me when she knew I was going to pitch. She couldn't just come there and wait for me to pitch in relief. So I called my mom and told her, I'm starting tomorrow."

"I didn't get a lot of great sleep," Behney says. "My first start was against Montreal, and I knew who the guys were only from the fact that I was a fan two years before that, and most of those guys were still playing at the time, so I recognized the names, but I didn't know how to pitch them. I didn't go through their lineup per se like I would if it was a normal start in the middle of the season. I knew they had a lot of left-handed hitters, and that's one reason why I was starting. That was Sparky's decision."

Having been with the club for less than a week, Behney had yet to find an apartment, so he walked to the ballpark from his downtown hotel. And what did he do to pass the time before his first major league start?

"I played chess with Larry Shepard. We played a lot of chess before the games, which was good. It had your mind working, but it wasn't about baseball."

Behney gave up just one run in the first four innings, but then in the fifth the proverbial wheels feel off.

"That's when they hit me," Behney says. "I had the bases loaded, two outs. They had one run in, and I think there had been an error. Tony Perez maybe. Then [Coco] Laboy hit a line drive into left field, and Bernie Carbo misplayed it. The other guys scored, and they took me out at that time. That was like $4\,^2/_3$ [innings], I think.

"I didn't think it was an exceptionally strong performance, but I didn't think it was bad enough that I shouldn't have at least maybe gotten another start. But that's not the way it worked out.

"You could definitely say I was not in command. I wasn't the type of pitcher that could go out there and have overpowering stuff where I could throw the ball down the middle and expect to get them out on a regular basis. Anybody can do it once in a while, but you can't do it on a regular basis. I was at a point where I was trying to throw strikes, and to throw a strike I was pretty much covering the plate more than I should have. You know how you hear you should work the six outside inches and the six inside inches? Well, I was working that middle part way too much. I didn't want to walk people, obviously, and I didn't have the command, maybe because I was nervous or whatever, but I didn't have the command that I was hoping to have.

"I think another one or two starts, and I would've known whether I was overwhelmed and couldn't get over it, or I just didn't have good enough stuff to pitch in the big leagues. Or maybe I did have good enough stuff, and I had to go through that learning process.

"That's the disappointing part," Behney says. "Like everybody else, give me five, six starts and let me find out, and then I'm okay with whatever happens, because then I know. Then I know I was a good Triple A pitcher and just didn't have the stuff to pitch in the big leagues. I never got a feel for whether I could compete or not compete. I just don't feel like I got enough opportunity to make that judgment. That was my high, that was my low, and that was my average."

Butch Metzger certainly saw success at the major league level. In 1976 Metzger pitched 123 $\frac{1}{3}$ innings for the San

Diego Padres over 77 games, 62 of which he finished. He posted an 11-4 record for the league's fifth best winning percentage, and ERA under 3, racked up 16 saves (also 5th best), and shared National League Rookie of the Year honors with Cincinnati Red Pat Zachary. But in 1977, his situation changed.

"I was the main closer for the Padres the year before," Metzger says, "and then they traded for Rollie Fingers, and Rollie Fingers, rightly so, became the number-one guy off the bat. I had gotten off to a pretty slow start, and I wasn't getting in some games, so they decided to give me a start to see if I could get on track. I started all through the minor leagues, so it wasn't like this major thing to be feared, so I said, Sure, I could do that. Anyway, it was kind of a short stint."

Metzger lasted just 2 $^2/_3$ innings against the Astros on April 23, 1977.

"I can definitely remember in that start some kind of strange, odd things," he says. "Like I remember two of those hits being pretty suspect, kind of blooper type stuff, like an outfielder, instead of running in and catching the ball, pulled up short and let it bounce. I can remember Roger Craig telling me, You didn't pitch bad enough to reflect what the box score said. He was pleased with the way I threw the ball, and I made some good pitches, but it's just one of those things. That's just the way baseball is.

"I remember being really frustrated about the whole thing, especially having thrown the ball and made much better pitches than the stats reflected. Nobody knows that other than myself and a couple of other people who witnessed it, and Roger coming up to me and trying to build me up a little bit. It was very frustrating, especially being a starting pitcher in the Coast League for two years in a row and leading the league in innings pitched and strikeouts, and to get my chance at a start and only go $2\,^2/_3$, I was like, Man, give me another chance. I know I can do better. But it just wasn't in the cards."

What Metzger found most strange was that he wasn't a starter all along.

"The biggest shock for me," he says, "was getting the chance in the major leagues and coming out of the pen. That was a little bit more foreign, and to be quite honest, when I was in Triple A with the Padres in Hawaii they told me they wanted me to come out of the pen as a closer, and I felt like I'd been demoted because the year before I pitched 204 innings and led the league. I'm thinking, Why are you doing this to me? Of course someone got called up early in the season, and I ended up being a starting pitcher after all and winning 15 games. I was 15 and 7 for Hawaii, doing my old workhorse starting thing again, and I'm thinking, Okay, I showed them. Now they won't do that to me again.

"Well, as you get older people say the chances of being in the starting rotation on your first opportunities in the big leagues are slim and none. You need to get real. You've got to come out of the pen and prove yourself, but in my case when I came out of the pen, it happened to be in kind of tight situations, and I did good three or four times in a row. Then they just kept feeding me the ball in closer and closer situations, and I think it was almost good that I didn't quite know what I was doing, because I just simply did everything the catcher said.

"I fell into it, and some people thought I had the right frame of mind for it because they nicknamed me Ho-Hum. I was pretty unemotional out there. If I walked two guys in a row I looked the same as if I'd just struck out two guys in a row. I was just trying to maintain a steady focus and concentrate on pitches and not get distracted by things. And it's hard. Sometimes you do get distracted, and it falls apart on you. Obviously my career didn't last that long. It fell apart on me on a regular basis towards the end there. I pitched myself right out of the big leagues like I pitched myself there."

Steve Ratzer's only major league start was also his major league debut—for the Montreal Expos on the last day of the 1980 season. The day before, the Philadelphia Phillies had clinched the National League East by defeating the Expos. For the players who had been in the majors all season, the game was essentially meaningless.

"I don't think I knew the night before," Ratzer says. "I don't think they told me. The season was pretty much over, and I remember waking up, just going to the ballpark, and when I got there Galen Cisco, the pitching coach, came over and told me that I was starting. He told me that. Dick Williams, the manager, didn't tell me. I was very happy to have an opportunity to finally pitch.

Ratzer had been with the Expos for nearly a month before his name was called. Though he'd been asked to warm up in the bullpen, manager Dick Williams never called his name.

"I remember going out there to pitch and them announcing my name, and it was kind of surreal," he says. "I don't know. It felt like there was like a haze inside Olympic Stadium, because my dream was always to play in the major leagues, and then I go out there and I'm warming up and they're announcing everything and they announce me as the starting pitcher. They had my stats from Triple A up on the scoreboard. I remember standing on the mound. They did the National Anthem, and I was on the field already, standing behind the mound, and I said a little prayer, talking to my parents who had been dead already, and, you know, not saying it out loud or anything, but just thinking, Dad, Mom, this is what I've always dreamed of, and I know you're watching me, that kind of thing."

If the pre-game introductions didn't provide enough drama, Ratzer soon found himself pitching to the man who would become baseball's all-time hit leader.

"Our whole team was basically a Triple A team out on the field behind me, and Bobby Ramos was my catcher. Pete Rose was my first batter. You figure that if our whole team's Triple A their whole team's going to be Triple A, but then Pete Rose is the first hitter. So I throw the first pitch of the game, a nice sinker, my best sinker, probably about 86, 87 miles an hour, low and away, my best pitch. He looks at it and turns around to Bobby Ramos and says, Man, this guy's got a good sinker. And Bobby calls time-out and runs out to the mound and he goes, Hey, Pete Rose says you've got a really good sinker. I said, Okay, let's throw it again. That was Pete Rose baiting me, of course. I threw exactly the same pitch, and he just hit a line drive between short and third like he did like 4,600 times in his career and stood on first base laughing at me."

The month of relative inactivity cost Ratzer. As a sinker-ball pitcher, he performed better when his arm was tired. He struggled through four innings, giving up five runs.

"I was a gamer," Ratzer says. "I was a guy that went out there and gave everything I had every pitch, every second. I was cheering for my team. I cheered the team the whole month of September. I didn't care that I wasn't playing. I wanted us to win."

Fellow minor league pitcher Hal Dues, who also sat for most of the pennant race, was one of those cheering Ratzer on.

"He said, Just go out there and show them what you can do. Show them. That kind of thing. Very supportive of the situation, and so was the whole team. The major leaguers didn't care, but the guys that I came up with, they all wanted me to do real well. They were all pulling for me very, very much.

"I don't think I candidly ever felt that pump, that craziness. I felt like I belonged in the big leagues. I felt like I could've helped the team win the pennant during the month. I guess the biggest question I had going into the game was, Can I get big league hitters out? There was that little bit of doubt in your head, but then I'm facing these guys that I got out all year. You know, I'm facing the Triple A guys that I played against because a lot of the guys were the Oklahoma City kids. If they had their regular lineup in there, it would've been a different thing for me, and I probably would've gotten some more adrenaline. The only thing was with Pete Rose. I calmed myself down just to throw and do what I could do to Pete Rose."

Right-hander Cliff Speck appeared in 13 games for the Atlanta Braves in 1986, his only major league season. He made his only start in San Diego on August 5, 1986. Speck had signed his first professional contract twelve years earlier, and before he made the majors had spent time in the Mets, Phillies, Orioles, and White Sox organizations.

"It's hard getting there," Speck says of his road to the majors. "I had some rib injuries early in my career. It's just gratification after however many years—I was almost thirty years old by the time I got there—the acknowledgment that I got there and I could pitch there. It's just nice to know you accomplished something after working hard."

"They told me I was going to start about twenty-five minutes before game time," Speck says. "They said, Start warming up. Zane Smith wasn't going to make his start. His elbow was bothering him or something. I don't remember. So I just started warming up, which is probably good because I didn't have time to think about it. I just went out there and started getting loose. Hadn't really thought about anything. Just kind of sitting on the grass beforehand, talking with the players and soaking in the vibrations that come out onto the field from the fans and whatnot, and went to work."

Speck worked 5 $^2/_3$ innings, giving up five hits and just one run in earning his first major league win.

Mike Armstrong was a first-round draft pick of the Cincinnati Reds in 1974. Twelve years after signing his first pro contract and six years after making his major league debut, Armstong got his first and only major league start wearing a New York Yankee uniform.

"It was September and they expand the rosters so they called me up. They were in Oakland, so I met the team there. Billy Martin was the manager, and Billy and I had had a kind of a history. Billy didn't care for me very much." Armstrong, of course, is not the only pitcher who felt that Billy Martin didn't like him.

"I think somebody had gotten hurt or somebody had a sore arm, and they needed a starter so they were going to throw me in there," Armstrong says. "It was as big a surprise to me as anything. I had been a reliever since 1978.

"When I was in the big leagues Billy didn't use me at all. I'd sit out there in the bullpen two or three weeks at a time, but when they finally sent me back to Columbus they said, You've got to get some innings in, so the best thing to do is to start you. So I started a few games. I didn't have much stamina or anything. I'd get along to the fourth or fifth inning and that was about it. When I got to Oakland they said, You're starting tomorrow, which really surprised me because here I was with Billy, who wouldn't let me pitch at all. He wouldn't even let me pitch an inning, and now I'm starting. I'm going, My gosh, what's going on here? And I probably put too much pressure on myself. It was an ugly outing."

Armstrong is not prone to exaggeration. He lasted 1 $^2/_3$ innings, giving up five hits (two of which were homers), two walks, and a total of six earned runs.

"Being on the Yankees," he says, "is a soap opera, and I think sometimes what happens to players is you get to be your own worst enemy in situations like that because you think too much. You wonder what's going on, and you worry. You're very easily distracted."

Armstrong slept little the night before.

"I was up trying to figure it out. Of course, there are no answers and no explanation for what some folks do. And so I started, and I didn't do well. I stayed up there until the end of the year because there was no place to send me back to. I sat around. Didn't do anything. Just vegetated out there.

"When I was in Kansas City I'd have a bad outing, and Dick Howser, the manager, made it clear—Look, you're going to have a bad outing, but this is a sum total thing. At the end of the year you're either an asset or you're not, but don't put all this pressure on one outing. With Billy, if you had a bad outing you just sat. It was a death penalty.

"He didn't handle pitching well," Armstrong says of Martin. "He was a brilliant strategist when it came to hit and run and stealing bases and pinch-hitting and all that stuff. There were very few that were as good as he was. But he didn't understand pitching. He didn't want to understand pitching. It was a nuisance to him."

(clockwise from top left) **DANNY BOONE, RAWLY EASTWICK,
AL HRABOSKY AND CESAR TOVAR** 158

8TH

Dock Ellis and the New World Order

In Los Angeles, Dock Ellis and I stop at a Fatburger. Dock is a baseball original, a former Pittsburgh Pirate pitcher best known for throwing a no-hitter on acid. This Fatburger, though, is not the original, Dock tells me. Dock is just back on red meat after his mother replaced turkey with ground round in his tacos.

"After you've been off the stuff for a while, you can smell it," Dock says. He offers the expression of a child who's just tasted liver for the first time. After one bite of the cheeseburger before him, Dock loudly hails the attention of the Asian cook behind the counter.

"Hey, man, this is not a Fatburger."

"Yes," the cook replies. "This is a Fatburger."

"Bullshit," says Dock. "You may have that Fatburger sign up there, but I've eaten Fatburgers and this is not a Fatburger burger."

"We use fresh meat patties," the cook protests.

"I'm not saying anything about your fresh meat patties. All I'm saying is that this is not a Fatburger burger."

The cook and Dock turn to face other business. "See, I

159

understand what he's saying, but he don't understand what I'm saying," Dock tells me.

This Asian grillman in a franchised Fatburger has no idea how much he and the institution of baseball have in common.

The antics of Dock Ellis have enthralled me since childhood. My obsession with the man goes much deeper than the average baseball fan who might view Dock as a perverse footnote in the annals of professional sports. This fascination, though abiding, has not been simple.

I grew up in Birmingham, Alabama, a fan of the Oakland Raiders in football and the Pittsburgh Pirates in baseball, the outlaws in black who always won in thrilling style. Like most of America, Birmingham operated without the blessing of a major sports franchise, but somehow the personalities of the cities of Oakland and Pittsburgh filtered down to me as working-class, a strong symbol for my hometown. If I could not cheer for a home team as friends from larger cities did, I would hold close to me the clubs from cities most similar to my own.

Although the Pirates were known as a team of free-swinging hitters, I knew by this point that pitchers controlled the game. Pitcher was the position I had chosen since good control and a precocious curve compensated for my own weak bat, but Pittsburgh's rotation hardly inspired the interest even tiny Freddie Patek, a utility infielder and one of the smallest men to ever play Major League Baseball, could instill. The Pirate pitching staff—

represented by such neutral types as Steve Blass, Bob Moose and Luke Walker—was, for the most part, a non-praiseworthy, white bread ensemble given the task of keeping the ballgame close.

And then there was Dock Ellis.

On the surface, a petulant, baby-faced black man from Los Angeles might seem to offer little for a young, white Alabama boy to identify with. True, he was a pitcher and he did display momentary flashes of brilliance, but Dock was also accused of letting the team down through what was described as "selfish behavior." Although I carried Dock's career in my memory for twenty years and his baseball card as my bookmark, not until this year did I realize why I latched on to Dock Ellis as my talisman.

I live these days in Dothan, Alabama, a city of 55,000 and a sense of isolation. After learning a hard lesson attempting to teach English at Enterprise State Junior College (alma mater of former Cubs' Rookie of the Year Jerome Walton) and its satellite campus on the Fort Rucker Army Base, I concluded that my life surely must have another end.

The first few weeks of the new year I applied for various part-time, minimum-wage jobs in the hope I could exchange a decent living for selfish moments to read and write, peace of mind, and freedom from the responsibility of dragging settled natives along a path they showed no interest in pursuing.

One morning, as I showered to interview for a job that would pay me $3.60 an hour to load and unload 110-pound bags of peanuts (the main industry here), I realized that I

DOCK ELLIS

had to find Dock Ellis. For all our differences, here was a man who refused to fit in, an outlaw, an unrepentant fighter. I had to know the survival rate for players like ourselves.

When I first spoke with Dock, I felt I had made a mistake. The man on the phone sounded much too slow to be the reckless fireballer I had envisioned, but I hadn't accounted for the West Coast time change. Dock's mother, who he lives with again in the same home where he was raised, had gotten him out of bed to answer the phone.

"Why are you interested in my career?" he asked. "Don't you know I'm dangerous?"

This is how the story goes: the Pirates fly into San Diego on a Thursday in May of 1970, the day before a series-opening doubleheader against the Padres. Dock checks into the hotel, rents a car, and drives to Los Angeles, where he drops acid and parties with friends. It is Friday afternoon when he realizes he is scheduled to pitch that evening. He takes another half hit of acid to keep himself awake and catches a plane to San Diego.

Dock arrives with just enough time to complete his warmup. A misting rain falls at Jack Murphy Stadium, and the game is sparsely attended, providing few witnesses for this peculiar bit of history.

The only video of the contest is one wide long shot, spliced and uneven, without audio, recorded by a single camera in the pressbox. The tape contains only the deciding pitch to each Padre batter. The camera does not follow balls hit out of the infield and no Pirate batters are shown.

The entire tape lasts less than twenty minutes and misses not only the final out, but the ensuing celebration as well.

The boxscore from the game does not do justice to its ugliness. Dock Ellis walked eight batters and hit one, loading the bases on two occasions in Major League Baseball's only no-hitter thrown on acid.

After lifting weights, Dock discovers he has lost the keys to his mother's house, so we move on to his sister's place, where he can take a shower. One nephew is sick and home from school.

"You ain't sick," Dock says.

"Yes I am, Uncle Dock."

Uncle Dock sounds a strange address to this man, but "daddy" would sound stranger, and Dock is, three times.

"You upstairs in your mama's room watching TV."

"I'm sick, Uncle Dock."

"What's that shit in your hair?"

"Curl activator."

"What do you want to look like a Puerto Rican for?"

The sparring is friendly but serious. Dock's nephew knows he's overmatched but looks for one good shot to gain his footing.

"I'll take you, Uncle Dock."

"When? When I'm in a wheelchair?"

"Yeah. I'll ram your legs in the wall."

While Dock showers I flip through the channels on the television downstairs. This is the day Marion Barry holds a press conference on his exit from drug treatment.

"Cokehead," Dock spews when he returns. "Look at him. Looks like he's been doing coke."

Mayor Barry asks the press not to come to his house, not to bother his family. "They were not elected," he says.

"Too quick," Dock says. "Too quick out of treatment to come out and talk shit. He didn't do the program right. He hasn't surrendered. The program says that I will be able to accept the things I cannot change, change the things I can, and have the wisdom to know the difference. And he don't know the goddamn difference. Let's go," he says. "Later, favorite nephew."

"Get out of here."

"I was gonna give you five dollars and now you dogging me. Dogging your favorite uncle just cost you five dollars."

"There'll never be another Dock Ellis in baseball," Dock says. "At least I hope not."

But Dock suffers no loss of pride and offers no apologies. Even more, he wants back in. Dock wants to be baseball's drug czar ten years after being its most notable user.

"I could be the drug and alcohol counselor for all of baseball," Dock says.

"Have you actually talked to someone in the league about doing that?"

"Oh yes."

"And the response was?"

"Oh no."

"Politely?"

"Oh no. They don't want to hear that shit. They cannot

control me. They're afraid of me."

Dock Ellis wants another chance at baseball, but he says, "Baseball will never hire me because they know that I'm no bullshit. I won't bullshit people, play their game."

"What about baseball bothers you the most?"

"The bottom line is, the way they treated me in baseball. It has manifested over the years. They knew I had a problem and never did anything about it. They didn't bring me up to the Majors when they should have. They were constantly trying to control me in all different ways, from where I went to who I associated with to the way I dressed and the way I combed my hair. All kinds of shit."

"So what makes baseball different from a regular job?"

"I don't know nothing about a regular job. I mean, I've had regular jobs, but baseball felt that I owed them something for letting me play. They allowed me to play because of my talent. That's all and I knew it."

"Do you owe baseball anything?"

"I don't owe baseball shit. I don't owe them shit. Hey, we used each other. That don't stop me from having animosity towards baseball, but I don't owe them shit, and they don't owe me nothing."

"But you're happy with who you are and baseball's a part of that."

"Why is baseball a part of me? I was destined to be who I am and known throughout no matter what I did. I had a predestination to be me. I could've been in politics and still been the same motherfucker. The same arrogant motherfucker. Charismatic individual, politician motherfucker."

"I'm not taking charisma away from you, but isn't a lot of what draws people to you the fact that you were an athlete?"

"True. But I could've done anything if I had used all of my energies."

"Did you put all your energy into baseball?"

"No. Not totally."

"Have you ever put all of your energy into anything?"

"In my recovery."

"So what's Dock Ellis's biggest success?"

"Ten years of sobriety."

"Is talking to people about drugs a part of your recovery or an extension of it?"

"Part of it. Sharing my experience, strength, and hope is part of recovery, to give it away. That's what they call giving it away."

Dock and I spend one day in Los Angeles checking on "the hoodlums," as he refers to them, borderline kids he's come across while helping out at the juvenile center in Pasa Robles. No one paid him for that work, and no one pays him to check on these kids now. Giving fits the man but not Dock's image. Talking to kids is part of what he's best at.

These hoodlums, however, know little of Dock's image. They don't know that Dock Ellis threw a no-hitter on LSD. They don't know that he played on two World Championship teams and they do not know that in 1971 he faced Vida Blue in baseball's first All-Star Game to feature two black men as starting pitchers.

As much as the no-hitter is mentioned, starting that All-Star game is the closest one can come to a defining moment in Dock Ellis' baseball career.

"The reporters asked me if I thought I should face Blue in the All-Star game because he was a given that year. I told them that baseball was too racist to let two black men face each other. They had to start me," Dock laughs.

The hoodlums do know that Dock played baseball and had problems with drugs, but the time he spends with them is devoted to other things than demonstrating how to throw a hard slider.

Scooter's mother, for example, called Dock because she was worried that all of her son's friends were gang-bangers. She didn't know how much longer he could stay out. Scooter's mom wanted Dock to talk to Scooter, so Dock and Scooter went for a drive, checked out the latest shipments at a local swap meet and, when they returned, Dock had one more pierced ear than when he left.

"Two is the in thing," Dock explained.

"Sometimes you wonder," Scooter's mother says, "who's influencing who."

But Dock knows more than "hoodlums" and family in Los Angeles. One afternoon we run into David Landers, the actor who played Squiggy on *Laverne & Shirley* and a long-time friend of Dock's. Landers is one of the few who actually saw the no-hitter.

At Fatburger Dock and I talk about Ron Howard and Michael Keaton and George Wendt. Dock spent time with all of them, in South America no less, during the filming of *Gung Ho,* a movie in which Dock played a small part.

"If I was on the other side of town, then we'd be running into all kinds of people. If I was to run into Michael Keaton then you would really hear some shit because I would be all over his ass. I told him what Hollywood was gonna do to his ass and he wouldn't believe me. His family's busted up.

"When I did the movie with him, I didn't trust him. Anybody born white that tells me they wish they were born black, I'm not gonna trust that motherfucker."

"He said that?"

"Yeah."

"What was his reason?"

"Something to do with where he grew up. You know he was raised right outside of Pittsburgh. His mannerism is black. With Michael, when we were doing that movie, I was with him for almost three months, and it was near the end before I really trusted him. But he was cool. I really like him now."

"But why did he want to be black?"

"I can't really pinpoint it. Had something to do with a DJ he listened to growing up. He's got that walk, you know, and he can't help it. He's got a hip to his walk and the way he talks. If he didn't say he wanted to be black, maybe he said that he thought he was black. Something like that."

"So how'd you get the part?"

"Ron Howard. They used to do those Hollywod star versus the press games before the Dodgers played, and I met him there when he was Opie. I was flying first class some-where, and I looked back and he was behind me and I said, 'What's going on, Ron?' and he said, 'Do I know you?' I told him, 'Man, fuck you. Fuck, you don't know me. I didn't say that shit to you when I met you.' Then he was all fucked up. When he was getting off the plane I handed him my card and he was like, 'Oh Dock, I'm sorry,'" and shit like that. But then I remembered that he didn't know me with a beard."

"Why do you tell people you were on acid when you threw the no-hitter?"

"Because it's the truth. It happened."

"If the point is to get people off of drugs, how glam-orous does it need to be? Doesn't mentioning the acid defeat the purpose?"

"No. Not if the story is told that when I took the LSD, I lost a whole day. The disastrous thing about that is, I lost a whole day."

"Sure, but a day out of someone's life to be one of two hundred men to ever throw a no-hitter . . . "

"Let's go back. I said I missed a day. Acid caused me to miss a whole day out of my life."

"But there are those who would say, 'Knock me out. Take April away from me,' just to pitch in a Spring Training game."

"What does that have to do with drugs causing me to lose a day? The acid caused me to lose a day. That's not glamorous. Then I realize I got to pitch and I throw a no-hitter. So what? I threw a fucking no-hitter."

"Come on."

"I happened to throw a no-hitter. I remember bits and pieces about it, but I threw a no-hitter. You can't take that away. I was fucked up, and I threw a no-hitter, but nobody can ever take that away. But you can't glamorize that. You can't say that that was a beautiful no-hitter. You've heard of ugly no-hitters? That was an ugly no-hitter. It was still a no-hitter, but something had to be wrong with this fucker throwing the ball all around the fucking stadium, hitting guys and shit, almost hitting them. Throwing one here and one over there and in the dirt and shit. Nolan Ryan didn't pitch that fucking wild."

"Squiggy says that most of the walks and the hit batter came after the fifth."

"I don't know. I've seen a scorecard, but I haven't looked to see when the walks and shit happened. I know it happened."

"So if I ask you if you had a no-hitter going and you were pitching around guys . . .?"

"Fuck no I wasn't pitching around no motherfuckers. I don't know what pitching around somebody means. I know now, don't let them hit nothing, but fuck that shit, pitching around some motherfucker. Now you got me going on this shit about some motherfucker trying to teach some motherfucker how to pitch. 'You got to pitch around them.' Pitch around who? Get the motherfucker out. I had Bob Veale slap me up against the head in a meeting because a man asked me, 'Dock, how you set the hitter?' 'I don't set no hitter up, man. What the fuck are you talking about?'"

"So it's all about power?"

"That's right. Kick ass and take names. All this fucking shit about teaching someone how to pitch. If you don't know how to pitch, get your ass the fuck out of Dodge. Now just throw the ball and hope they don't hit it. Pitch around some motherfucker. I hear these motherfuckers talking on TV, Palmer and them, talking about pitching around some motherfucker. He used to pitch around motherfuckers. It happens but I never knew nothing abut it. Maybe if I did I would've won more games, but those hitters knew I was coming after them with everything I had."

"But you got offended when I brought it up."

"The reason why is because you used the term 'pitch around.' 'Pitch around' is a term to get out of shit. You're saying that the walks in my no-hitter could've happened because I was pitching around guys and that set me off. You can ask anybody. Everything I threw was hard. You either kick their ass or they'll kick yours."

Dock is forty-five now and he's been into weight training for about a year and a half. Lifting weights, he says, takes up idle time and requires discipline, both strong needs fulfilled for someone in recovery. But Dock's idea of his image plays a big role in his motivation as well.

In Los Angeles Dock works out at Muscle Express, a converted warehouse on Long Beach Boulevard in the middle of Compton. Music so tinny it sounds wrapped in aluminum foil comes from a jambox placed next to half-finished changing rooms. The area is furnished with one sink, one toilet and a solitary bench that looks like it's been repossessed from a Little League dugout. The surrounding walls are plywood panelling. The gym is spacious and the noises of a weight room reverberate over a thin layer of crimson indoor/outdoor carpet. Even the mirrors, everpresent in weight rooms, are spaced. Dock points out the various men who enter.

"I'm gonna do my arms his size. V-shaped. Gotta work on this belly. They get on me about my sit-ups."

The belly is small by most forty-five-year-old standards and only sticks out on Dock because the rest of his body is so lean. Just the tiny beginnings of crow's feet hinting at his true age.

The environment is different in Florida. At the Gold Coast Gym in Pompano Beach, Dock pays his seven-dollar workout fee to a young woman, maybe twenty-two, tanned and leotarded. The crimson carpet here is much thicker, nearly as plush as a downstairs surburban playroom. Mirrors cover the walls and to get to the weight benches one has to pass through a maze of computerized bicycles. More women are present at this facility, and it goes without saying that the average age skyrockets over the Muscle Express. Only one other black man shows in the two hours we are there, and this gym has recently gone to twenty-four hours a day, an impossibility in Compton, where citizens escape the streets before dark. At Gold Coast, Dock is referred to as "Brown" after the World Wrestling Federation's Bad News Brown. Even here Dock carries something about him that stands out—the walk, the temperament, the demeanor that shows that he is somebody.

"I was on the phone in the lobby the other day and I said, 'Hold on, man, we're on television. And it was this Bad News Brown. The haircut, the earring, everything. I mean, the dude looks just like me.'"

From what I've seen on television, Dock's in better shape, if not quite as large as the wrestler. Dock's stomach is flatter at least. He talks about his sit-ups, but I never see him do them. Dips are also listed on his daily workout schedule and he avoids them, even in conversation.

"How come you don't do those dips, Dock?"

"Man, those things hurt."

What brings Dock Ellis to Pompano Beach, a sleepy stretch of Atlantic Beach so filled with retired folk that hotel bar bands cover "Feelings" by design, is the hottest story of this Spring Training.

Dock is here to "counsel" Pascual Perez, a former Atlanta Braves pitcher, nicknamed "I-285" after missing a scheduled start because he was unable to successfully exit the interstate loop around the city to get to the ballpark. George Steinbrenner signed Pascual for close to two million dollars a season one year after he posted a 9-13 record with Montreal and now, with Spring Training under it tightest schedule ever due to the owner's lockout, Pascual Perez's appearance at camp is over a week past due.

The story making the rounds is that Perez was detained at the airport in his native Dominican Republic by a paternity suit filed by a woman with whom he already has one child out of wedlock. His delay also causes unvoiced speculations of drug use since Perez has already had two cocaine-based run-ins with the law during his career. The combination of the Yankees, George Steinbrenner, Pascual's unique personality, two million a year and now Dock forms an instant story. The beat writers have been circling for a week, waiting for Pascual's appearance. The Yankee pitching coach wears a button that simply asks, "Donde?"

The Yankees have placed Pascual in Pompano Beach rather than the team's facility in Fort Lauderdale to keep him out of the limelight. He is, in effect, in hiding. So Pascual has been complaining about the remoteness of his accomodations. Specifically he is not close enough to the malls for his liking, especially since he is still without a driver's license. But that, of course, is also the point. Dock and Pascual's management team would like to keep him away from the press until things have quieted down, so he and Dock can "focus," a big word here, on a plan.

Pascual, Dock and I are having breakfast in the hotel lounge and, as luck would have it, USA Today has a graph in this morning's paper listing the highest-paid and highest-rated baseball players by position.

Pascual is listed for a million this year even though his contract is for much more. Charlie Liebrandt, the Braves' most recent pitching acquisition, is making over a million a year, more than Tom Glavine, John Smoltz and Pete Smith combined.

"I bet Charlie Liebrandt isn't pitching five hundred ball over the last three years," I say. "And that's with a winning

team." In my mind are the Braves' injured-and-out pur-
chases of Bruce Sutter, Andy Messersmith and, worst of all,
Len Barker.

"Shit," Dock says. "You pitch .500 ball and I'll get you
two million a year. Isn't that right, Pascual?"

Pascual Perez does not appreciate the joke.

The skies are clear with absolutely no chance of the rain
South Florida so desperately needs. At 9:30 in the morning,
a full three hours before the scheduled start of today's exhi-
bition game, as many as seventy fans crowd the gate to the
already full player's parking lot. It is Pascual who must wave
to the gatekeeper for our car to be let in, but it is a wave of
dismissal.

"Let us go, beetch," Perez says, annoyed. Everything is a
"beetch" this morning—the male gatekeeper, the twenty-
minute drive to the park, the stiffness in his shoulder from
throwing the day before.

"I don't want to throw today. You got to talk to them,
Dock."

But here Dock knows his place and shows uncharacter-
istic diplomacy. He knows he's not been brought in as a
pitching coach.

"They're scared of you, man. They think you're a wild
man doing all that crazy shit and stuff. Tell 'em you need a
day off."

Pascual's "crazy" is no match for the pair's other topic
of conversation, Cesar Cedeno, a former outfielder with
the Houston Astros. Dock and Pascual have been searching

for mutual acquaintances within the world of baseball; after all, Dock retired the same season Perez came up to the big leagues. A plethora of Cedeno tales form a bridge: Cesar screaming at managers, Cesar screaming at fans and UCLA co-eds screaming at Cesar, which follows from a discussion of the dicksize of several Dominican ballplayers.

"Sonofabitch was almost late," Dock tells me after delivering Pascual to the Yankee clubhouse. "He told me he had to be here at nine-thirty, but that's what time practice starts. We should have been here at nine."

"Isn't this a little like babysitting?" I ask, knowing Dock's image of himself would never allow him to admit it. But the day before I lost track of Dock. He had taken Pascual for a haircut that somehow lasted four hours, and then to Hooters, a kind of sports bar without the sports where the waitresses wear halter tops and dayglo orange running shorts. The food is basically hamburgers and chicken wings and this was Pascual and Dock's second trip to the restaurant in Pascual's three nights in Florida.

The little-boy syndrome that Dock mentioned has been in front of me all day long. Dock maintains that baseball players will have problems with drugs directly proportional to the average American except for the "little-boy's syndrome."

"We're patted on our back and butts our entire lives because we're special when it comes to playing ball. And the closer it gets to the time when that's all over, we take something to fill the gap."

So isn't it wrong to treat Pascual this way, cater to him?

Dock spends twenty minutes with a member of Team de Pascual, as they're calling themselves, discussing who will go to New York to find Perez a place to live.

"He's got somebody to find him a place to live?" I ask.

"He doesn't have a driver's license and all ballplayers have people find them a place in New York," Dock says. "I had a guy find me a place complete with directions to the ballpark. It's a big city."

"What about the haircut? Would you have taken Pascual for a haircut if he had a driver's license?"

"Hell no," Dock says and walks away.

Dock doesn't see his handling of Pascual Perez as an audition for baseball. He doesn't forsee any problems for Perez even though he insists 20 percent will fall back regardless of what counseling is provided.

"I told you. Baseball will not hire me because they know I will not bullshit people."

"Well, tell me what your plan is."

"Can't do that," Dock says.

"Why not?"

"'Cause it'll be published and, the next thing you know, it'll be implemented."

"So what's wrong with that?"

"I won't be part of it," he says.

"But it'll be documented as your idea. You help people for free. You don't think there's any chance you'll be hired by baseball. If you're going to help these guys anyway, and you won't be hired to implement the program, then what's the point in holding your ideas back?"

"That makes sense," Dock says. "That makes sense. I'll tell you. I believe that if a guy gets busted or comes forward—they now say that he has to come forward but I don't give a shit if they come forward or not—they should be given a chance to go to treatment."

"Once a problem is acknowledged."

"Right. I feel, though, that they should miss baseball for a whole year, a whole year. And that the insurance policy for baseball players should cover more than just a twenty-eight-day treatment program. I believe they should go in the program for six to nine months. Say six months and let that six months be devoted to aftercare. Something they can carry over to a baseball season."

"How much do they get paid the year they're off?"

"They don't get nothing."

"Let me play devil's advocate. You come to me and say, 'I saw you smoking dope outside the San Diego locker room, outside the Cincinnati locker room and now you're swinging late on curve balls . . . '"

"We're not talking about swinging late on curve balls. I would not allow them to use on- the-field performance as a basis for deciding someone's on drugs. There are people who drop fly balls who only drink milk. You know, Dale Murphy's not the best outfielder in baseball and all he'll drink is milk."

"I'm not going bankrupt, my wife still loves me, and I'm playing well . . . "

"The clubs know who uses drugs. You document and

then confront them. I don't care if you're hitting .500 and got five hundred homeruns and five hundred RBIs. If you get busted for drugs, you're gone. You did it, you're sick."

"But don't they resist?"

"Of course they resist. That's part of the process. But the year off is not punishment; it is to get the person's life together where they do not depend on baseball. But you have to get an agreement from the owners and the Players' Association and neither one will stand with me on that. And the other reason, besides the year, that they will not deal with that, is because they, and I mean the owners, is because they're drunks. And so many front office people are drunks. You go to the winter meetings and all you see are drunks. Deals are made when people are drunk. Writers write about 'how could they make this deal?' Because they were drunk. One organization takes advantage of another one because they drink too much."

"When we started you said that you didn't want to talk about your plan because baseball would take it. Now you say that the owners and and the players will never go along with it."

"They will take from it and do something with it. They did it in Atlanta. I took a whole proposal to Hank Aaron, and he tells me he don't handle this. Now where in the hell is the shit that I gave him? In their drug program. I networked the whole thing for the entire minor leagues for the Atlanta Braves."

* * * * *

I'm back home in Dothan now, and Dock is off doing whatever it is Dock does when he doesn't have an audience, which is rare, I think. I've decided to go to a temporary employment agency so one Friday morning I rise early, shower, shave—I'll leave the haircut for a real job—and put on a button-down and a pair of khakis. I go to the agency that has the most ads in the newspaper. They don't charge a fee and it's temporary I tell myself, a nice outlook for my relationship with Dothan.

There are two doors at the agency: one is marked Industrial Division and one is marked Clerical. With my background in English, I decide to go through the clerical entrance. After all, I'm out of my jeans, and in the back of my mind is an ad offering work "plucking, deboning, eviscerating and otherwise preparing chicken for market." I don't want to be talked into that one since chicken is one of my diet's staples. I have to think that there probably aren't many people who need that job who know the meaning of the word "eviscerating."

I wait alone in the clerical reception area for fifteen minutes, hearing voices behind a hall door, before I decide to knock.

"Oh, you're not supposed to be in here," the woman said.

"Why not?" I asked. At another office, a woman would not let me apply for a secreterial position ostensibly because I was male.

"We just do bookkeeping in here," she said. "You need to go next door."

So next door I went, a bit tired and confused about the set-up. I didn't need this job. I wasn't starving.

"How are you today?" the woman behind the desk asked. There were three of them in all, bouncy and smiling in matching bright pink T-shirts with the company logo emblazoned across the chest. This could've been the Amway of temp agencies. "Can I help you?"

"Yes," I said. "I'd like to fill out an employment application."

"I'm sorry, sir. We don't take applications on Fridays."

Their ad said nothing about not taking applications on Fridays. They were open. Three pink-shirted employees were filing. Why couldn't I fill out an application? Why didn't they take applications on Friday? They were an employment agency. Their lifeblood should be taking applications.

I stayed long enough to explain to the woman why I wouldn't be back on Monday as she suggested. I was there then and if she wouldn't take my application, well, that was it. I got up in her face, so to speak. Dock would've been proud of me, I think.

But on my way to the parking lot I realize that, at forty-five, Dock is missing the fastball that allowed him to command listeners to his version of the story. He no longer has the power that commanded enough attention to get the start in an All-Star Game or the talent to command significant change in his world. What baseball wanted from Dock is gone.

I'm younger than Dock, true, but I do not have the walk. I do not have the swagger. What I'm missing this Friday, as I walk away from a temporary employment agency in Dothan, Alabama, is a fastball.

9TH

The Lists

Hall of Fame—Starting Pitchers

Grover Alexander (1938)
Chief Bender (1953)
Mordecai Brown (1949)
Jim Bunning (1996)
Steve Carlton (1994)
Jack Chesbro (1946)
John Clarkson (1963)
Stan Coveleski (1969)
Dizzy Dean (1953)
Don Drysdale (1984)
Dennis Eckersley (2004)
Red Faber (1964)
Bob Feller (1962)
Rollie Fingers (1992)
Whitey Ford (1974)
Pud Galvin (1965)
Bob Gibson (1981)
Lefty Gomez (1972)
Burleigh Grimes (1964)
Lefty Grove (1947)
Jesse Haines (1970)

Waite Hoyt (1969)
Carl Hubbell (1947)
Catfish Hunter (1987)
Fergie Jenkins (1991)
Walter Johnson (1936)
Addie Joss (1978)
Tim Keefe (1964)
Sandy Koufax (1972)
Bob Lemon (1976)
Ted Lyons (1955)
Juan Marichal (1983)
Rube Marquard (1971)
Christy Mathewson (1936)
Joe McGinnity (1946)
Hal Newhouser (1992)
Kid Nichols (1949)
Phil Niekro (1997)
Jim Palmer (1990)
Herb Pennock (1948)
Gaylord Perry (1991)
Eddie Plank (1946)

Old Hoss Radbourn (1939)
Eppa Rixey (1963)
Robin Roberts (1976)
Red Ruffing (1967)
Amos Rusie (1977)
Nolan Ryan (1999)
Tom Seaver (1992)
Hilton Smith (2001)
Warren Spahn (1973)

Don Sutton (1998)
Dazzy Vance (1955)
Rube Waddell (1946)
Ed Walsh (1946)
Mickey Welch (1973)
Hoyt Wilhelm (1985)
Vic Willis (1995)
Early Wynn (1992)
Cy Young (1937)

Cy Young Winners

Johann Santana (AL, 2004)
Roy Halladay (AL, 2003)
Barry Zito (AL, 2002)
Pedro Martinez (NL, 1997/AL 1999, 2000)
Pat Hentgen (AL, 1996)
John Smoltz (NL, 1996)
Randy Johnson (AL, 1995/NL 1999, 2000, 2001, 2002)
David Cone (AL, 1994)
Jack McDowell (AL, 1993)
Greg Maddux (NL, 1992, 1993, 1994, 1995)
Tom Glavine (AL, 1991, 1998)
Bob Welch (AL, 1990)
Doug Drabek (NL, 1990)
Frank Viola (AL, 1988)
Oral Hershiser (NL, 1988)
Roger Clemens (AL, 1986, 1987, 1991, 1997, 1998, 2001, 2004)

Mike Scott (NL, 1986)
Bret Saberhagen (AL, 1985, 1989)
Dwight Gooden (NL, 1985)
Rick Sutcliffe (NL, 1984)
La Marr Hoyt (AL, 1983)
John Denny (NL, 1983)
Pete Vuckovich (AL, 1982)
Fernando Valenzuela (NL, 1981)
Steve Stone (AL, 1980)
Mike Flanagan (AL, 1979)
Ron Guidry (AL, 1978)
Randy Jones (NL, 1976)
Catfish Hunter (AL, 1974)
Jim Palmer (AL, 1973, 1975, 1976)
Gaylord Perry (AL, 1972; NL, 1978)
Steve Carlton (NL, 1972, 1977, 1980, 1982)

Cy Young Winners *(continued)*

Vida Blue (AL, 1971)
Fergie Jenkins (NL, 1971)
Jim Perry (AL 1970)
Tom Seaver (NL, 1969, 1973, 1975)
Denny McLain (AL 1968, 1969)
Bob Gibson (NL, 1968, 1970)
Jim Lonborg (AL, 1967)
Mike McCormick (NL, 1967)
Dean Chance (ML, 1964)

Sandy Koufax (ML, 1963, 1965, 1966)
Don Drysdale (ML, 1962)
Whitey Ford (ML, 1961)
Vern Law (ML, 1960)
Early Wynn (ML, 1959)
Bob Turley (ML, 1958)
Warren Spahn (ML, 1957)
Don Newcombe (ML, 1956)

STEVE CARLTON (NL Cy Young Winner: 1972, 1977, 1980, 1982)

SANDY KOUFAX (NL Cy Young Winner: 1963, 1965, 1966)

Gold Glove Winners—Starting Pitchers

Year	NL	AL
2004	Greg Maddux	Kenny Rogers
2003	Mike Hampton	Mike Mussina
2002	Greg Maddux	Kenny Rogers
2001	Greg Maddux	Mike Mussina
2000	Greg Maddux	Kenny Rogers
1999	Greg Maddux	Mike Mussina
1998	Greg Maddux	Mike Mussina
1997	Greg Maddux	Mike Mussina
1996	Greg Maddux	Mike Mussina
1995	Greg Maddux	Mark Langston
1994	Greg Maddux	Mark Langston
1993	Greg Maddux	Mark Langston
1992	Greg Maddux	Mark Langston
1991	Greg Maddux	Mark Langston
1990	Greg Maddux	Mike Boddicker
1989	Ron Darling	Bret Saberhagen
1988	Orel Hershiser	Mark Langston
1987	Rick Reuschel	Mark Langston
1986	Fernando Valenzuela	Ron Guidry
1985	Rick Reuschel	Ron Guidry
1984	Joaquin Andujar	Ron Guidry
1983	Phil Niekro	Ron Guidry
1982	Phil Niekro	Ron Guidry
1981	Steve Carlton	Mike Norris
1980	Phil Niekro	Mike Norris
1979	Phil Niekro	Jim Palmer
1978	Phil Niekro	Jim Palmer
1977	Jim Kaat	Jim Palmer
1976	Jim Kaat	Jim Palmer
1975	Andy Messersmith	Jim Kaat

Year	NL	AL
1974	Andy Messersmith	Jim Kaat
1973	Bob Gibson	Jim Kaat
1972	Bob Gibson	Jim Kaat
1971	Bob Gibson	Jim Kaat
1970	Bob Gibson	Jim Kaat
1969	Bob Gibson	Jim Kaat
1968	Bob Gibson	Jim Kaat
1967	Bob Gibson	Jim Kaat
1966	Bob Gibson	Jim Kaat
1965	Bob Gibson	Jim Kaat
1964	Bobby Shantz	Jim Kaat
1963	Bobby Shantz	Jim Kaat
1962	Bobby Shantz	Jim Kaat
1961	Bobby Shantz	Frank Lary
1960	Harvey Haddix	Bobby Shantz
1959	Harvey Haddix	Bobby Shantz
1958	Harvey Haddix	Bobby Shantz
1957	Bobby Shantz **only one listed for 1957*	

GREG MADDUX
(14-time Gold Glove Winner)

JIM KAAT
(16-time Gold Glove Winner)

188

Most Valuable Players—Starting Pitchers

YEAR	NATIONAL	AMERICAN
1986		Roger Clemens BOS (24-4 / 2.48)
1971		Vida Blue OAK (24-8 / 1.82)
1968	Bob Gibson STL (22-9 / 1.12)	Denny McLain DET (31-6 / 1.96)
1963	Sandy Koufax LAD (25-5 / 1.88)	
1956	Don Newcombe BRO (27-7 / 3.06)	
1952		Bobby Shantz PHI (24-7 / 2.48)
1945		Hal Newhouser DET (25-9 / 1.81)
1944		Hal Newhouser DET (29-9 / 2.22)
1943		Spud Chandler NYY (20-4 / 1.64)
1942	Mort Cooper STL (22-7 / 1.78)	
1939	Bucky Walters CIN (27-11 / 2.29)	
1936	Carl Hubbell NYG (26-6 / 2.31)	
1934	Dizzy Dean STL (30-7 / 2.66)	
1933	Carl Hubbell NYG (23-12 / 1.66)	
1931		Lefty Grove PHI (31-4 / 2.06)
1924	Dazzy Vance BRO (28-6 / 2.16)	Walter Johnson WSH (23-7 / 2.72)
1913		Walter Johnson WSH (36-7 / 1.14)

10 Greatest Seasons by a Starting Pitcher

We must step away for a while, but please feel free to talk among yourselves. We'll even give you a topic—top ten seasons by a starting pitcher in a leading role since World War II. Here's our list:

YEAR	PITCHER	RECORD	ERA
2000	Pedro Martinez	19-9	1.74
1968	Bob Gibson	22-9	1.12
1999	Pedro Martinez	23-4	2.07
1985	Dwight Gooden	24-4	1.53
1997	Pedro Martinez	17-8	1.90
1964	Dean Chance	20-9	1.64
1978	Ron Guidry	25-3	1.74
1966	Sandy Koufax	27-9	1.73
1953	Warren Spahn	23-7	2.10
1964	Sandy Koufax	19-5	1.74

Rookie of the Year—Starting Pitchers

National League

2003	Dontrelle Willis (Florida)
2002	Jason Jennings (Colorado)
1999	Scott Williamson (Cincinnati)
1998	Kerry Wood (Chicago)
1995	Hideo Nomo (Los Angeles)
1984	Dwight Gooden (New York)
1981	Fernando Valenzuela (Los Angeles)
1979	Rick Sutcliffe (Los Angeles)
1976	Pat Zachry (Cincinnati);
1975	John Montefusco (San Francisco)
1972	John Matlack (New York)
1970	Carl Morton (Montreal)
1967	Tom Seaver (New York)
1957	Jack Sanford (Philadelphia)
1949	Don Newcombe (Brooklyn)

DONTRELLE WILLIS

American League

1981	Dave Righetti (New York)
1976	Mark Fidrych (Detroit)
1968	Stan Bahnsen (New York)
1963	Gary Peters (Chicago)
1961	Don Schwall (Boston)
1955	Herb Score (Cleveland)
1954	Bob Grim (New York)
1952	Harry Byrd (Philadelphia)

DAVE RIGHETTI

GARY PETERS

ABOUT THE AUTHOR

The author with Elrod Hendricks

Rob Trucks is on the thin side of handsome, a veritable pole vault stanchion of a man. He is the author of *Cup of Coffee: The Very Short Careers of Eighteen Major League Pitchers* (Smallmouth Press, 2003) and *The Pleasure of Influence: Conversations with American Male Fiction Writers* (Purdue University Press, 2002). He lives and writes about baseball, literature and music for *Spin*, Newsweek.com, *BookForum, East Bay Express, Philadelphia Weekly, San Diego CityBeat, Cleveland Scene, Baltimore City Paper, Boulder Weekly,* and *Houston Press,* among other publications, from his closet-sized apartment in Long Island City, NY, but longs to move to Albany so he can truthfully call himself an Albanian.

BOOKS OF INTEREST

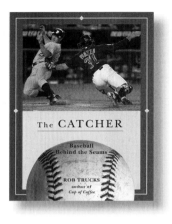

The CATCHER
From the Baseball Behind the Seams *series*
By Rob Trucks

The Catcher. Burdened by protective gear, squatting in the dust behind the plate, target for foul tips and fastballs. Although he wears "the tools of ignorance," the catcher is the quarterback of the baseball diamond, calling the pitches and pitch-outs, the only player with a view of the entire field of play.

The Catcher is the first book ever to cover this crucial position in such astonishing depth. Through interviews with several generations of major league catchers, you'll learn how they got started at the position, their most memorable plays, and the techniques they mastered to become great catchers. You'll hear first-hand what it's like to catch a no-hitter and a knuckleball, and how it feels to be battery mates with Tom Seaver, Steve Carlton, Juan Marichal, Nolan Ryan, Jim Palmer, Greg Maddux, and many other pitching greats.

Author Rob Trucks talked with more than fifty major league catchers, past and present—Yogi Berra, Lance Parrish, Charles Johnson, Ed Bailey, Frank House, Elrod Hendricks, Andy Seminick, Mike Lieberthal, Michael Barrett, and more. Their insightful accounts give you a never-before-seen glimpse into life behind the mask.

Paperback   **Price $14.99**
ISBN: 1-57860-164-9

To order, call: 1.800.343.4499 / www.emmisbooks.com
EMMIS BOOKS 1700 MADISON ROAD CINCINNATI, OHIO 45206